Culture in Law Firms

Best Practices for Engagement and Retention in a Hybrid World

Authors
Naomi Beard Nelson, Mary Ellen Connerty and Michelle Egan

Managing director
Sian O'Neill

***Culture in Law Firms: Best Practices for Engagement and Retention in a Hybrid World*
is published by**

Globe Law and Business Ltd
3 Mylor Close
Horsell
Woking
Surrey GU21 4DD
United Kingdom
Tel: +44 20 3745 4770
www.globelawandbusiness.com

Culture in Law Firms: Best Practices for Engagement and Retention in a Hybrid World

ISBN 9781787429284
EPUB ISBN 9781787429291
Adobe PDF ISBN 9781787429307

Table of contents

I. Introduction

1. Bounce forward, not back

If you are still trying to wrap your head around what we all experienced these past few years, you're not alone. "What has happened is a once-in-a-century transformation of our work environment."[1] In March 2020, there was a sudden shift to working remotely. Now we are at a crossroads, trying to navigate what law firm life looks like in a hybrid work era, and there is no roadmap, precedent or industry best practice to guide us.

Moreover, the constant stress triggered by the pandemic has changed people. Lawyers have shared that they are less committed to, and fulfilled by, the profession and fewer law graduates say they want to go to a Big Law firm.[2] While the Great Resignation appears to be over, at least based on turnover rates, the lack of loyalty to employers remains.[3] "That's colliding with a push [by some in the industry] to return to previous ways of working and thinking."[4] It is critical that we do not allow ourselves to revert to how it was. We need to bounce forward, not back. There is a permanence to the shift, and the stakes are high if we don't create a new normal that satisfies the unique circumstances of the four generations in the workplace.

Layer on the increasing importance of artificial intelligence (AI), which has been described as "an absolutely transformative moment in the practice of law", and we are truly at the dawn of a new era.[5] The capabilities of generative AI are mind-blowing and the professional duties and responsibilities that accompany this new technology have yet to be ironed out.[6] New AI practice groups are being formed, clients are seeking counsel on its use and firms are grappling with when and how to use the technology themselves.[7] The potential to upend the makeup of the law firm workforce also looms large.

According to O'Melveny chair Brad Butwin: "The challenge for the legal industry is to thrive in the face of change of unprecedented speed and scale – some of it foreseeable, some of it not."[8] And "moving a traditionally risk-averse organisation through [all of this] change is not easy".[9] Moreover, the antiquated business model of law firms remains profitable, limiting the motivation to make changes, coupled with the fact that law firms continue to face other significant challenges, including a competitive talent landscape, an exhausted, mentally unhealthy workforce, and pressure to control costs amid a possible economic downturn.[10] Firms will have to have the humility to listen and to learn – and be willing to put the work in.[11]

2. Whatever the new normal is going to look like, it has to be designed

So what should we do to ensure that law firms and their lawyers and

What has emerged in all of the noise is that culture is paramount when it comes to retaining top talent and maximising performance. After all, one constant in all of this is that a firm's working capital is its people. Firms must be intentional, thoughtful and diligent as they cultivate and redefine who they are and what matters to them.

professionals thrive in these uncertain times? What has emerged in all of the noise is that culture is paramount when it comes to retaining top talent and maximising performance. After all, one constant in all of this is that a firm's working capital is its people. Firms must be intentional, thoughtful and diligent as they cultivate and redefine who they are and what matters to them. Loyalty is not gone – it is going to be given to firms that prioritise their people, and leverage their values, make them explicit and truly embody them. It is also important not to rush to find solutions, but to acknowledge that this is a moment when much is in flux, when piloting small fixes and experimenting with them will be more efficient and successful than trying to create a 100% designed solution. Despite the uncertainty, the good news is that there are established successes in how to cultivate firm culture that can lead us in the right direction.

3. Culture currency

The word 'culture' often gets thrown around and can seem hard to articulate, leaving it vulnerable to being cast aside. Gary Burnison of Korn Ferry defines it well:

> *Culture is the way an organization gets things done. It propels people from me to we, from self-interest to shared interest. It's the organisational atmosphere enveloping purpose, vision, values, assumptions, behaviours at scale – and ultimately results. It fills the white space around formal plans, structures, systems, mindset and abilities – in short, it's an organization's everything.*[12]

Culture is essential to a law firm's success and should remain firmly embedded in strategic planning. When people have guideposts and feel that their work has purpose, they are more productive, collaborative, and committed to their firm's success. Firm culture also fosters relationship building, promoting loyalty and retention of top talent.

Clients also demand as much. They seek to partner with firms that have shared values and that they know they can trust.

4. The role of culture in changing work environments

Complacency (and reversion) can easily undermine the strides toward positive culture development that were taken by law firms during the height of the pandemic.

Pause and consider whether your culture is aligned with the new realities of the time.[13] If it isn't, you will need to redefine it for a hybrid world.[14] Firms were able to maintain – and even expand and improve – connections between colleagues during the pandemic. Acting with intent and using new technology, showing empathy for what others were going through and using a more personal touch – all this enabled firms to foster a real sense of connection. We need to continue to lean on these tools and tactics as we continue to redefine what working at a law firm looks like in this hybrid time. Firms willing to embrace changing norms and evolve their cultures will continue to thrive.

The importance of cultivating a sense of trust and transparency is also critical. Firms that share information in real time, and acknowledge the unknown and the challenges being faced – rather than waiting until the messaging is polished and all of the kinks worked out – build a sense of trust and appreciation among their workforce. Continuing this approach of openness and authenticity is essential to maintaining a robust culture.

Keep in mind that what culture looks like at each firm can (and should) be different. Some cultures are hard driving, some are collegial – each approach can work. So long as firms have core convictions – know who they are, who they want to be, what they do, and do it well – they will be poised for success.[15]

Firms best positioned to navigate the future are employing strategies that:

- identify the elements of their cultures that have to change to carry them forward, while being true to their fundamental principles and ethos;
- practice versatile, inclusive and evolved leadership;
- embody their values at all levels of leadership;
- use transparent, inclusive communication;
- carefully design training, mentoring and feedback programmes;
- focus on well-being and mental health; and
- demonstrate an awareness and sensitivity to external geopolitical factors and the growing polarisation of society and the workforce.

The six elements of law firm culture

While the current period is an opportunity for all of us to think differently, it remains the case that effective functioning in the following six areas is most essential to cultivating culture building:

- leadership and communication;
- developing people;
- well-being and flexibility;
- relationships, engagement and collegiality;
- diversity, inclusion and belonging; and
- recruiting and onboarding practices.

What constitutes 'effective' has evolved and must continue to be honed and reevaluated.

5. What's in this report?
Referencing the six areas above, in the following sections we study the critical elements of building and proactively nurturing law firm culture, including:

- the evolution of leadership and communication;
- engagement and people programmes in a hybrid environment;
- holistic well-being and flexibility;
- relationships, engagement and collegiality;
- the current state of diversity, inclusion and belonging in light of recent court decisions and the politicisation of D&I; and
- changes in recruiting and onboarding practices.

In each section we look at how the dynamics of hybrid work environments and generational differences (pay particular attention to your Millennials) may impact decisions about developing new cultural norms.

6. Global application
While much of the research and commentary in this report reflects the current status of law firm culture in the United States because this is our area of expertise, the practices and lessons learned can be applied worldwide. Law firm culture is not bound by geographic constraints. Adjustments may be needed to accommodate legal, cultural and corporate practices in a particular place, and the geopolitical forces at work in your area, but the mission is the same: create a thriving firm culture and your people, your clients and your firm will thrive.

II. Leadership and communication

1. What it is and why it matters

As new tensions rise over what being in the office looks like in terms of flexibility and generational expectations, a leader's role in cultivating firm culture has never been more critical. Diversity and inclusion consultant Lauren Stiller Rikleen, founder and president of the Rikleen Institute for Strategic Leadership, aptly noted in a *Law360* article:

> *One of the things that law firms have to do a better job at is understanding that it's a people business, and managing people well is the single most important job of a leader in any organization.*[16]

Having the right leaders is especially important now. In the face of so much change, leaders need to be very intentional about how to engage with groups of people, while advancing growth and productivity. It is a unique skill set and leading effectively in this uncertain time is difficult.

Leaders who consciously adapt their approach to managing in this new era and focus on culture will find their lawyers and professional staff more receptive, content and motivated. And they will stay. A renewed sense of loyalty will follow, as firm cultures evolve to better align with the priorities of their people.

Firm leadership sets the tone and articulates and models the norms which define a law firm's culture. Leaders "translate vision and values into policy, practice ... and daily behavior".[17] This requires that leaders at all levels, including practice group leaders, office managing partners and senior associates and counsel must not only promote new behaviours, they must also embrace and model them – they must walk the talk. Their support in implementing policies and programmes that respond to their people's post-pandemic expectations and aspirations is critical. The extent to which each lawyer and professional staff member enacts the firm's norms and values in their interactions with colleagues determines the strength, cohesion and consistency of the culture over time.

2. Considerations in a hybrid work environment

Since experiencing remote work, "[e]mployees have become more empowered" and many have grown accustomed to an expansion of resources, flexibility in their schedules and autonomy in where and how they want to work.[18] They know now firsthand that what they were told was impossible (working at home) is not only possible, but productive – professionally and personally.[19] This has generated a new power dynamic and poses a challenge for firm leaders who are accustomed to setting the rules.[20] In addition, many senior lawyers and leaders agree with the flexible approach and want it for themselves. "The leaders most likely to succeed are those who learn to interact differently with their teams and employees" and shape their policies to embrace the new hybrid environment, rather than resist it.[21] Hybrid work can be a lose–lose or a win–win. It is here to stay. Take the time and make the effort for it to win – create a policy that meets the business needs of a firm, while respecting lawyer and professional staff needs and preferences.

2.1 Listen well and listen often

In the hybrid era, team members will have fewer opportunities to connect with colleagues and build relationships face to face. As a result, according to David Liddle, CEO and chief consultant at The TCM Group, "people often miss out on important context, subtle nuances are lost and there's less chance to pick up on the body language cues that indicate how people are feeling".[22] The potential for miscommunication and misunderstanding is also much greater than in an exclusively physical environment.[23] Dr Larry Richard, founder and principal consultant at LawyerBrain LLC, told *The American Lawyer* that firm leaders need to "demonstrate 'deep listening' – put simply, have the ability to not just repeat what someone says, but how they feel".[24] Listening well and listening often are keys to reducing the chance of confusion.[25] To understand what their people need to succeed in the office as well as remotely, leaders need to intentionally create opportunities to listen carefully in the context of both.

2.2 Proximity bias awareness

"Hybrid teams also need to be aware of proximity bias – the tendency for partners or those distributing the work to reward the people with whom they interact in person."[26] Cozen O'Connor executive chairman and CEO, Michael Heller, recently formalised this preference (albeit not without qualification – see note 27), stating that Cozen "will encourage partners to give work to those who are in office".[27] However, such policies seem to miss what we have learned. The past few years have shown us that people can thrive and be productive in both settings. Leaders need to be adept at managing and creating equity in both in-person and hybrid environments, investing in systems that will track the distribution of work so as not to inadvertently exclude remote and hybrid lawyers. This system should include how work flows to new partners as well. Intentional and formalised work streams ensure that those down the hall aren't given special access to work. Failure to ensure this jeopardises the development and retention of those not in the office as often. Moreover, proximity bias may disproportionally impact women and under-represented groups, who tend to prefer flexible arrangements more often than their white male counterparts.[28]

Leaders need to be adept at managing and creating equity in both in-person and hybrid environments, investing in systems that will track the distribution of work so as not to inadvertently exclude remote and hybrid lawyers.

3. Generational opportunities

Firm leadership should also be mindful of the impact that generational differences are having on the workplace. While generalisations can be problematic, each generation entered the workforce under certain conditions, which ultimately helped to shape its sense of purpose, its preferences and its drivers for success.[29] A firm that is able to tap into generational differences "to invigorate, attract and retain talent is [at] a competitive advantage".[30]

3.1 Four generations in the office

Keep in mind that "[f]or the first time in modern history, there are four separate generations co-mingling in the workplace, and each has prevailing mindsets that have collided in the pandemic era".[31] To bridge this gap, "savvy law firm leaders will elevate generational understanding to a strategic level", according to Marcie Borgal Shunk, president and founder of The Tilt Institute.[32] They will take time to understand the priorities and concerns of each generation and look for ways the groups complement each other. They will pay close attention to how they lead and revise their expectations for how their colleagues may respond.[33] Smart leaders will find ways to celebrate each generation.

For discussion purposes (and acknowledging this is not an exact science), we are defining the four generations in the office as:

- Boomers: 1946–1964;
- Generation X: 1965–1980;
- Millennials: 1981–1996; and
- Generation Z: 1997–2012.[34]

Table 1: Workforce numbers in the United States, 2020 (%)[35]

Boomers	18.6
Generation X	34.8
Millennials	38.6
Gen Z	6.1

Keep in mind, the oldest members of Gen Z are now 26. This means the percentage of lawyers represented by this generation is likely much less than 6.1% of a law firm's workforce – though Gen Z should not be ignored. With over 10,000 Boomers per day reaching the age of 65, by 2030 Generation Z will constitute about 30% of the workforce.[36]

3.2 New way of leading

"[L]eadership styles under the ... Boomer generation were different than they are now."[37] Boomers worked hard and then were expected to work harder, and risked being kicked out if they did not follow what they were told to do.[38] Boomers and some Gen Xers also rose through the ranks in environments where workers had to prove themselves and 'earn' the right to have a say on big issues.[39] That is not the view of younger lawyers, according to Shunk.[40] Millennials seek more involvement in the process and desire to have more input into decisions.[41] "That's a shift in perspective from the 'earn your way' mentality," she says.[42] Younger lawyers want to remove some of the hierarchy.[43]

With regard to Gen Z, as a group they are more entrepreneurial, diversified and individualistic than prior generations.[44] Like the Millennials before them, Gen Z employees value flexibility and care for their mental health.[45] For this generation, leading by example through vision and feedback is crucial.[46] Feedback should go both ways, fostering an environment of open dialogue and understanding.[47]

Firm leadership needs to be proactive in running firms differently. This is not a shift in style, it is a new way of leading. Chris Cebollero, leadership specialist and author, has commented: "The days of command and control and leading from a position of authority [are] over."[48] Putting the workforce first through inclusion, engagement and active listening has emerged as the new way to lead.[49] Failure to adapt to the new normal may estrange a critical mass of today's workforce.

4. Change management

Before we get into the specifics of best practices for leadership today, let's explain what we mean by change management and what the process entails. Organisational change management is "concerned with the people side of change".[50] It is a structured approach to ensuring that changes are smoothly and effectively implemented, and that lasting benefits are achieved.[51] This is easier said than done. There are lots of models that overlap and diverge. The key is to have a roadmap. One model was created by leadership guru John Kotter in 1996, based upon analysis of 100 different organisations going through change.[52] His research highlighted eight key lessons, which he converted into a practical eight-step model:[53]

1. Create a sense of urgency
2. Build a guiding coalition
3. Form a strategic vision
4. Enlist a volunteer army
5. Enable action by removing barriers
6. Generate short-term wins
7. Sustain acceleration
8. Institute change

Employees want to feel heard, understood and considered as firms make decisions about the organisation as a whole and their own personal development.

Although originally represented by Kotter in a linear fashion, it is better to think of the steps as a continuous cycle to ensure that the momentum of change is maintained.[54]

4.1 New way of leading

People management must be at the forefront. It takes effort and it is not an area which many law firms are used to prioritising, or considering strategic. Leadership must appreciate the scale and scope that effective management requires. They must be intentional, versatile and inclusive in how they lead. It is increasingly important that law firm leadership demonstrate authenticity, adaptability, transparency and accountability from the top down.[55] Employees want to feel heard, understood and considered as firms make decisions about the organisation as a whole and their own personal development.

4.2 The versatile leader

What has emerged during the pandemic, and as we adjust to hybrid work models, is that versatility is a strong component of effective leadership in this uncertain time.[56] Versatility is regarded as "the ability to read and respond to change with a wide repertoire of complementary skills and behaviours".[57] Some situations need leaders to "take charge, force difficult issues ... and make tough decisions, while others require leaders to enable, support ... and include people".[58] Sometimes leaders need to focus on future strategic direction, other times on day-to-day operations.[59] Versatile leaders "deftly toggle between" (at times) opposing behaviours and styles.[60] They are able to "read the room and adjust their behaviour accordingly".[61]

Most leaders are better at one set of behaviours and "tend to over-rely on them at the expense of complementary behaviors".[62] This creates blind spots and limits their versatility.[63] Thankfully, research suggests that versatility is largely a learned capability and there is not a single personality profile that corresponds to versatile leadership.[64]

In the past, firms chose leaders for their core strength; some served as motivators and strategic thinkers, while others rolled up their sleeves and got in the weeds. Firms now need leaders who can do both. Leaders who can draw upon different skill sets are crucial: they need to adjust to the style needed in the moment and be able to make the tough decision, all while hearing out the room.

Table 2: Proportion of overall leadership effectiveness related to versatility[65]

Year	%
1997	35
2008	50
2020	63
2022	55

Despite the benefits of versatile leadership, a recent reduction in its effectiveness (see Table 2) may signal a bounce back by some to outdated ways of leading. Ensure that your leaders are not reverting to old practices rather than embracing a more agile way to lead.

4.3 The inclusive leader

Five behaviours of inclusive leaders

Inclusivity is another central component of effective leadership. Wei Zheng, Jennifer Kim, Ronit Kark and Lisa Mascolo have identified five key behaviours that help leaders make their organisations more inclusive:[66]

- Prioritise authenticity and psychological safety (see section 4.3(a), below), viewing the two as essential building blocks for creating an environment where people can express themselves freely and share dissenting views without fear of retribution.
- Redefine rules rather than unquestioningly following them; be willing to challenge outdated customs and seek ways to detect practices that exclude certain groups of people, and replace them with new ones that give greater access to under-represented groups.
- Embrace active learning and consistent implementation, acknowledging that the effort to be inclusive is learned, rather than passively acquired.
- Ensure equal opportunity and equitable outcomes.
- View inclusive leadership as everyone's responsibility, not just a human resource one.

The numbers speak for themselves. "[I]nclusive leaders see a 17% increase in team performance, a 20% increase in decision-making quality, and a 29% increase in team collaboration."[67] Inclusive leaders also reduce employee attrition risk by 76%.[68]

(a) How to create psychological safety

Creating psychological safety is a core task of the inclusive leader.[69] That means lawyers and professional staff "feel comfortable admitting mistakes, disagreeing with the team leader and asking questions".[70] When you commit to that type of environment, trust is built and information flows more freely, which is a competitive advantage.[71]

Keep in mind that psychological safety isn't the default.[72] Harvard Business School professor Amy Edmondson has said that psychological safety "should not be considered the norm ... [C]reating and maintaining it takes deliberate practice".[73] Leaders are often oblivious to the fact that they create threats. For example, a manager who is "distracted during a one-on-one meeting with an employee could [unintentionally] create a threat for that person, making them feel like they [are not] receiving their boss's full attention".[74] Minimising and eliminating those threats takes constant work in the moment and, when possible, in advance. If the manager is likely to be distracted, they could say to the employee, "I'm going to be looking down at times to check my phone because I'm waiting for a call from my doctor's office."[75] Even seemingly small adjustments and acknowledgements can have a significant impact.

4.4 The evolved leader

In addition to honing versatility and inclusivity, there are several other approaches leaders should take when guiding their workforce in this new era.

(a) Be empathetic

According to Dr Larry Richard, lawyer, psychologist and founder of LawyerBrain, "the pendulum is swinging in the legal industry in the direction of leaders who are 'highly empathetic' and more emotionally intelligent".[76] Leaders who "demonstrate empathy and support for their teams create a nurturing work environment".[77] Taking the time to acknowledge the individual needs, goals and challenges of colleagues builds strong relationships based on understanding and compassion.[78] This is instrumental in building firm culture and retaining talent. Many leaders are finding that "if they can't find ways to treat their young talent as individuals, they are increasingly likely to lose them".[79] Stepping into this new way of leading will take work, often with several missteps along the way, but it is essential to shepherding the next cohort of lawyers.

(b) Be an ear at the table

According to Jacob Engel, CEO at Easyhire, effective firm leaders have also shifted to becoming a voice at the table – not *the* voice.[80] They need to go a step further, to becoming an ear at the table. Leaders should listen carefully and actively consider the thoughts and ideas of others.[81] People want to feel validated for their opinions.[82] When a decision is ultimately made, it is important that firm leaders demonstrate they have taken those opinions into account.[83] And they want to feel safe to express them. "When people have the chance to make even small decisions, they feel like they have 'skin in the game,' a feeling that keeps them engaged and striving toward a collective outcome."[84] This creates a sense of purpose and unity for the team. In turn, teams will respond with a greater willingness to support and implement the task at hand – developing new loyalties to the firm. By way of example, Hogan Lovell recently launched a programme called HL Voice, where the firm plans to hold six-monthly check-ins with their people to learn what is top of their minds, what is working well, and what is not working well.[85]

(c) Invite everyone to the table

Breaking down the division between lawyers and professional staff should continue as well. The old approach to maintaining a sense of hierarchy receded rapidly during the pandemic, and this was a positive boost to overall morale. Firms have more widely embraced the fact that it is only when all people within their organisations are included that a cohesive and strong sense of culture can take hold and flourish. When everyone – lawyers as well as professional staff – is invited to take part in the conversation, leaders will find that even if an employee does not agree or understand, it will be approached from a position of respect and care. Moreover, creating the space for colleagues to hear and learn from the experiences and perspectives of everyone in the office creates a shared experience and demonstrates that decisions are made taking everyone's circumstances into account.

(d) Encourage and embody a growth mindset

Another important component of effective leadership is cultivating a growth mindset, not only as a leader, but for those you lead as well. "Mindsets are leaders' mental lenses that dictate what information they take in and use to make sense of and navigate the situations they encounter," explain Ryan Gottfredson, professor at California State University-Fullerton, and Chris Reina, assistant professor at Virginia Commonwealth University.[86] They drive what leaders do and why, and are foundational to how leaders think, learn and behave.[87]

A mindset refresher

- **Fixed mindset:** This is believing that your qualities are carved in stone. It creates an urgency to prove yourself over and over. You only have a certain amount of intelligence, a certain personality and a certain moral character. ("Failure is the limit of my abilities." "I'm either good at it or I'm not." "I don't like to be challenged." "When I'm frustrated, I give up." "Feedback and criticism are personal.")[88]
- **Growth mindset:** This is based on the belief that your basic qualities are things you can cultivate through your efforts. Everyone can change and grow through application and exercise. ("Failure is an opportunity to grow." "My effort and attitude determine my abilities." "Feedback is constructive." "I am inspired by the success of others." "I like to try new things.")[89]

People with a fixed mindset avoid challenges, lose interest when the work gets hard and give up easily.[90] It makes them feel like they aren't talented or smart.[91] They let one setback define them forever.[92] According to Breeann Webster of Dame Leadership, a leader with a fixed mindset can be detrimental to the organisation, believing that their knowledge and expertise are sufficient to solve a problem.[93] They may avoid seeking input from their team, dismiss alternative ideas, resist change or become complacent.[94] This can suppress creativity and hinder an organisation's ability to adapt to new challenges.[95]

Those with a growth mindset seek out and thrive on challenge because they know that they will grow and learn.[96] They don't let a single outcome define their ability or potential.[97] Extensive research has found that leaders "with a growth mindset are more mentally primed to approach and take on challenges, take advantage of feedback, adopt the most effective problem-solving strategies, provide developmental feedback to subordinates, and be effortful and persistent in seeking to accomplish goals".[98] In essence, a growth mindset enables them to perform in their roles more effectively.[99] And a leader's mindset "significantly affects the team's performance and the overall growth of the organisation".[100]

Leaders also need to cultivate teams where growth mindsets can flourish. The reality is that our mindsets likely exist on a continuum, with some combination of growth and fixed mindsets.[101] As a result, psychologists are now focusing on mindset as a cultural feature in organisations, how our environments can trigger a growth or fixed mindset, and the role managers and colleagues play in shaping our mindset.[102]

David Rock, CEO of the NeuroLeadership Institute, advises that leaders should "openly discuss and model resilience, which is a hallmark of a growth mindset".[103] He also advocates that leaders be proactive about helping others identify and transform their mindsets. Rock suggests that using the simple word 'yet' can achieve this. For example, "I am not a technology person yet" shifts their entire perspective to one of growth.[104] It is also important to value progress, embrace experimentation and learn from others.[105]

4.5 This applies to all leaders

While we continue to reference firm leadership in our discussion, it is essential that all leaders within the organisation's structure embrace the importance of a new way of leading. The approaches outlined here need to be reinforced down the line – with office heads, practice group leaders, partners, counsel. Anyone managing people needs to understand the priority of people management and to be trained on how to practise it. Make leadership part of their job description and be clear and intentional about what is expected of them. The boots-on-the-ground leaders have a huge impact on the development of young talent and the future of the firm.

4.6 Support your leaders

Because so much is expected of leaders now, support and guidance are also crucial. And leaders need to be open to feedback and growth opportunities, and to have constant self-awareness and awareness of others.

The firm's leadership cannot be the only voices. They have to be able to rely on office heads, practice group leaders, the entire professional development team – a whole cohort of leaders who together help to reinforce communication and keep it alive. Empower other leaders to keep the conversation going. If you don't, you will see a drop in engagement.

4.7 The clear communicator

The pandemic reinforced the importance of transparency, authenticity and accessibility in communication in order to maintain a strong culture. Ignore these aspects at your peril:

> *Law firm leaders who don't adapt their communication styles – particularly moving away from top-down, old-school 'tough guy' talk – to a changing workforce risk alienating workers and enduring unwanted backlash.*[106]

Tolerance for this outdated style has rapidly declined.[107]

"Clear and open communication is [also] essential for building trust and loyalty within a team."[108] And using an authentic, caring tone, maintaining a regular cadence of outreach, and evincing a genuine understanding of the needs of your people is essential to building trust. Law firm leaders should also actively listen to concerns and feedback from all firm professionals.[109] Successful firm leaders ensure that the entire workforce is included in all communications and that information is shared fully across the whole organisation.

4.8 How and when to communicate

Lawyers are trained to make their work perfect before it is shared. Perfection is not the goal when it comes to internal communication. We learned from the pandemic that people need to hear what is happening in real time – the good, the bad and the ugly. There is authenticity in sharing when it isn't perfect or all figured out – messages will be received with greater openness and trust.

Leaders also get into trouble when they communicate something and think they are done. Communication has to be a daily skill, continuously honed. Leaders need to communicate matters constantly in rotation, so different aspects of a firm's values stay top of mind. The content needs to be future focused and reinforce a sense of collective mission. Firms also need to find multiple pathways in concert, through annual 'state of the firms', townhalls, video messages, emails, voicemails and so on.

Another essential component of effective communication hinges on all leaders within the firm adopting the same message. The firm's leadership cannot be the only voices. They have to be able to rely on office heads, practice group leaders, the entire professional development team – a whole cohort of leaders who together help to reinforce communication and keep it alive. Empower other leaders to keep the conversation going. If you don't, you will see a drop in engagement.

4.9 Communication preferences

Another important element to successful communication is to talk openly to one another about preferences, particularly when it comes to methods of communication.[110] Hybrid work and generational differences impact how and when messages will be best received for each individual. When new teams are formed, establish communication practices at the outset. Consider who will be working remotely some (or all) of the time. Who prefers to meet in person? Is email, Teams, Zoom or phone best? Who has time-off plans coming up? All of this upfront communication helps teams run better and team members feel cared for.

4.10 Space for new (Millennial) leaders

Another important focus for law firm leadership is the development of future leaders at the firm.[111] Scott Westfahl puts it bluntly: "If you've got baby boomers at the helm of your organisation, you've got a talent gap coming."[112] Moreover, "[r]esearch has shown that most law firm leaders are a generation older than the generation of CEOs and executives running their biggest clients".[113] Gen Xers may seem like the natural next choice.[114] However, many of that group have been rethinking their life priorities and nearly half are actively considering early retirement.[115] This means that it is time to focus on your Millennials.

There is a good chance that newer Millennial partners and senior associates will be ready for leadership earlier than existing firm leaders may typically think.[116] With many of their counterparts in other industries already occupying seats at the table, there is a business case for these moves as well. It's important to examine your leadership pipeline and invest the time and effort now, including by upskilling, to position these new leaders for success.[117]

(a) Prepare and make space

To prepare for this next cohort of leaders, firms need to position themselves as attractive organisations for this group to lead. For Millennials, this means focusing on making long-term commitments to inclusion, sustainability, ESG and diversity, inclusion and belonging (DIB) efforts, and a larger overall purpose.[118]

Firms will also need to make space for Millennials to assume leadership roles. One way to create space for new leaders is to establish a custom of leadership role rotation for practice, office, or department leaders, so that being rotated out of a position after a few years is no longer stigmatised as a forced departure.[119] This also enables your firm to build a more diverse, inclusive bench.[120]

Hybrid work and generational differences impact how and when messages will be best received for each individual. When new teams are formed, establish communication practices at the outset.

(b) How to find them
Identifying the right new Millennial leaders is also critical. Make sure they understand the importance of culture and are forward looking in their approach to management. Looking at a firm's review processes (performance reviews and upward reviews) is a great way to begin the process of identifying future leaders and start to fill your bench. Where there is intersection amongst the various reviews, there are your potential future leaders. When managers and peers respect them – and subordinates as well – it's a winning combination.

(c) Talent discussions
Once you have begun to identify future leaders, take the time to have meaningful talent discussions separate from performance reviews. Get firm leadership and the relevant partners in a room and figure out as a group where the leadership needs are, who is capable and what they need to get there.[121]

Firms should create leadership frameworks and consciously develop and continuously assess future leaders against these metrics. One talent assessment tool is a standard nine-box grid, with one axis for potential and the other for performance.[122] As Kalley Anderson, director of marketing at Kevala (formerly of Trackstar), says: "Performance refers to [a potential leader's] current performance

Table 3: Potential/performance grid[124]

POTENTIAL				
	HIGH	Experienced employee capable of an expanded role; may sometimes require coaching and/or mentoring.	Performs extremely well in current job and has the potential to do more; this employee should be given stretch tasks to help them develop to the next level.	Performs consistently well in a variety of tasks. This is your 'superstar' employee: a motivated, big-picture thinking, problem solver.
	MEDIUM	This employee could progress within their current level with coaching and stretch targets.	This employee may be considered for an expanded role at the same level, but may need coaching in, eg, people management.	Current role may give opportunity for growth and development. This employee may benefit from help with strategic thinking.
	LOW	Consider whether this employee should be reassigned to a lower level or exit the organisation.	This employee is an effective performer but may have reached full potential. Consider coaching employee to develop skills to think laterally and become more innovative.	A high-performing, experienced employee who has reached limits of potential. Still valuable to the company, however, and could benefit from developing communication and delegation skills.
		LOW	MEDIUM	HIGH
		PERFORMANCE		

at their current position, Potential refers to their ability to learn a new task and incorporate their skills into higher-level positions."[123] Potential leaders are plotted into the boxes, and from there moved into succession plans.

(d) Succession planning

Your talent review process has identified and evaluated the next generation of leaders, and now you can put a succession plan in place for each critical role to ensure the firm can continue to operate and serve its clients should people leave.[125]

Many firms use the following categories when mapping out the timelines for potential candidates:

- Emergency Replacements;
- Ready Now;
- Ready 1–3 Years; and
- Ready 5+ Years.[126]

Emergency Replacements ensure that a firm is prepared, if there is an unexpected absence or departure. Ready Now and Ready in 1–3 or 5+ years let a firm plan for when talent needs arise. The process also identifies talent gaps and risks, and when external candidates should potentially be considered.[127]

Some lawyers may resist succession planning because of the implication that they are replaceable.[128] The concern may be that planning for succession somehow weakens the lawyer's relationship with clients or their position in firm leadership.[129] However, "[w]hen done properly, a succession plan benefits the individual lawyer, clients, colleagues and the firm as a whole".[130] It can be effective for building teams that support firm operations and ongoing client relationships.[131] It also gives clients peace of mind to know that their go-to lawyer has an adequate support network available to provide ongoing services.[132]

"Legal industry observers say succession planning remains a weak spot for smaller firms, often leading to a firm's dissolution when a key leader retires."[133] Founders of small firms should get younger lawyers involved in leadership and direct client work sooner, if they intend to keep the firm going.[134]

(e) Getting (Millennial) leaders ready

The next step is to develop the bench and prepare them for future leadership roles. Future leaders can be trained in a number of ways. The best programmes start with the self, which enables real transformation and a substantial boost in mental health and well-being.[135] This, in turn, can foster improved engagement and effectiveness. It is a whole-person approach to growth. It is less about learning specific, tactical skills than it is about cultivating the broad capabilities (eg, self-awareness or resilience) necessary to adapt to dynamic and evolving challenges.[136]

How, where and for how long are also important. "Don't underestimate short, intensive programmes."[137] Research shows that shorter programmes can yield surprisingly outsized improvements. A two- to four-day intensive programme can have the same or even greater impact than an equivalent four-week programme, saving on time and cost.[138]

Also, embrace online learning. Research suggests that in many situations, development can happen just as effectively online as in person. It's lower cost, more efficient and can reach a much larger audience. Lastly, the most effective programmes build on initial programmes "with reminders and other ongoing interventions designed to establish long-term habits and continued engagement".[139]

Firms will see the best results by using a suite of resources available, and should choose approaches that work best for their culture and budget, in alignment with the younger generation's learning preferences.

4.11 Key takeaways

Leaders set the tone and enact firm culture. In order to walk the talk, focus on:

- listening actively;
- creating equity amongst those in the office and working remotely;
- raising awareness of and adapting to generational differences;
- leading with versatility, inclusivity, authenticity, empathy and a growth mindset;
- empowering all leaders – office heads, practice group leaders, partners, counsel;
- communicating clearly and consistently; and
- making space and preparing for new leaders.

III. Developing people

1. What it is and why it matters

The importance of professional development in creating a thriving law firm culture cannot be emphasised enough, and it has never been more critical than it is today. According to leaders at Gartner Human Resources, burnout, exhaustion and career insecurity have eroded performance,[140] and law firm leaders are "starting to wonder if they have at least three years' worth of undertrained associates who didn't benefit from the professional development historically gleaned from in-office exposure to how legal work gets done".[141]

Even where firms have provided extensive online training programmes, industry experts have observed that "some things are missing, like how to maneuver or negotiate in a live environment".[142] The result is that some lawyers fail to learn the skill set appropriate for their class year.[143] Equally concerning is that law firm recruiters and talent professionals report that little has been done to patch the holes in newer associates' education and development.[144] Rather than intentionally tackling the specific shortcomings that have been identified, more senior lawyers bemoan the situation but do not help to create specific learning interventions to close the gaps. And firms, in general, have fallen back on time-tested training approaches. It's not too late to change direction on this.

After such an upheaval in training for so many lawyers, refocusing on professional development is key to driving engagement and productivity. It is also critical to a firm's long-term success.

Firms that invest in the growth of their people demonstrate a genuine commitment to cultivating the advancement of the lawyers and professionals who work there, creating higher overall job satisfaction and morale.[145] Law firms with carefully focused professional development programmes are also more likely to attract potential talent eager to advance their careers. And programmes should be offered in a hybrid format, remotely and in person to reach the broadest audience most cost effectively.

2. Considerations in a hybrid work environment

As we know, a lawyer's initial years of practice are similar to those in other master–apprentice relationships.[146] Yet hybrid work limits newer lawyers' opportunities for what Paul Schmidt, chair of BakerHostetler, has referred to as a kind of "active osmosis" – absorbing what someone is doing or saying:[147]

> *If you're an associate watching a partner on a conference call, you're learning their style, listening to their questions and listening to a client's responses.*[148]

When the call ends, there's often a natural segue to additional questions.[149] In a hybrid environment, this lack of observational learning *could* be a real a hindrance in a lawyer's development. However, it doesn't have to be. In this example, an associate could just as easily have been part of a Zoom meeting, or listened to a phone call, to learn from a partner – followed by an intentional conversation to confirm what the associate learned and whether they have any questions. Innovative firms will think about how they are going to replace 'active osmosis' and create talent development programmes that provide other channels for associates to learn these skills.
By identifying and responding to the changing needs of their organisations, professional development departments can continue to play an essential role in strengthening culture in the face of hybrid challenges.

2.1 Upstream digital hesitation

There is a continuing concern that junior lawyers hesitate to ask questions and seek feedback in a hybrid environment. While working remotely, senior lawyers freely call on junior lawyers on an as-needed basis, but junior lawyers do not feel the same comfort level to go upstream and interrupt more senior lawyers with what might be regarded as trivial questions or concerns.[150]

It seems as though everything has to be scheduled, and that is an impediment. You don't need an appointment. It is important to encourage and normalise remote contact, even for minor questions, to ensure that associates aren't trying to tackle problems on their own that would be approached collaboratively in person. It is as simple as encouraging associates to pick up the phone and ask for help.

It is also more challenging for a junior lawyer to seek impromptu guidance than was historically the case when a more senior lawyer tended to sit a few offices over.[151] There is an inefficiency with having to schedule online meetings rather than informal office visits.[152] Coordinating days in office can help create the opportunity for the walk-down-the-hall moments.

There also needs to be motivation for more junior lawyers to come into the office. Practice groups, departments, affinity groups and professional development departments could plan in-office training or discussion sessions on topics that will bring people in and facilitate relationship building, learning and collaboration.

2.2 Opportunities for advancement

There may be advancement concerns for lawyers who utilise remote and hybrid work. Partners may be more likely to push for a promotion an associate with whom they observe and interact on a daily basis, as opposed to an associate they only see sporadically in person.[153] Raising awareness about this potential partiality could help minimise its impacts.

The onus is on everyone to make sure that all lawyers get equal access. Associates can't sit at home and wait for the phone to ring, and counsel and partners need to engage all their team members, regardless of where they sit. Robust talent reviews will also help ensure that all lawyers' contributions are acknowledged and considered.

Future-focused law firms strive to be places where there are meaningful opportunities for those utilising a hybrid schedule. From an engagement and retention point of view, flexibility is what existing and top incoming talent expects and seeks. Firms are most likely to attract and retain this talent if they do have a true hybrid model that is accepted and promoted. Remember, to win as a firm, you have to win the talent war, and happier, more engaged teams are more productive and serve clients better.

2.3 The new role of the office

While maintaining flexibility will be important in attracting and retaining talent, law firms can also communicate to their lawyers the

There also needs to be motivation for more junior lawyers to come into the office. Practice groups, departments, affinity groups and professional development departments could plan in-office training or discussion sessions on topics that will bring people in and facilitate relationship building, learning and collaboration.

advantages of working in person.[154] It is essential that in-office time be productive and collaborative; otherwise, lawyers will quickly realise that sitting alone in their office on Zoom behind closed doors is pointless (and much more time consuming with a commute) than doing the same thing at home.

Firms need to explore what else will bring people in. Some are encouraging in-office attendance by making a few adjustments to their physical spaces. Law firms are going beyond offering free food (this still works too) and are getting creative with their floorplans to find new uses for free space offered up by hybrid work schedules.[155] Some firms are adding amenities and collaborative spaces in an attempt to draw lawyers back to the office. These improvements include cafés, 'genius bars' for tech support, lounge areas and exercise rooms. Smaller and midsize firms are taking a more customisable approach and are utilising their extra space to offer new recruits 'partner-size' offices.[156]

Beyond physical adjustments, firms should also consider offering speakers and workshops on topics that matter to their workforce, such as wellness, well-being and *pro bono* projects. Rather than demand a return, innovate and find ways to make people want to be there.

It is also important to revisit old traditions that may have been on pause for the past few years and use them as reasons to be in the office to reinforce those cultural elements; for example, diversity days, wellness fairs, affinity group meetings, promotion celebrations and welcomes for new associates. People come to the office because they want to see each other. Find your 'glue' events to bring people in and create meaningful connections.

2.4 Set an example by coming in – and by asking

Keep in mind that the benefits of in-person interactions only work for newer associates if their managers make the same commitment.[157] More seasoned lawyers can get most of their work done remotely, but if their offices are empty, it is difficult for the newer lawyers to benefit from making the effort to come in.[158] There is a tension, though, for more senior associates and newer partners as the pressure for billing means that avoiding commutes and minimising time spent interacting with colleagues can be ways to be more efficient and productive.[159] Reminding this cohort of the importance of associate development for the benefit of their own projects and the long-term development of the next generation of lawyers may help shift this mindset.[160] The benefits of being in the office work best for more junior lawyers when their managers are there as well.

Managers also shouldn't forget that when they need people in the office for important reasons, they can simply ask them to come in. When there is a need, people will come.

3. Generational considerations

The four generations in the office may have something in common after all – everyone's social skills have deteriorated since 2020.[161] Moreover, "[n]o one, from any generation, has cracked the code for navigating our new shared professional environment",[162] and this is especially problematic for those who entered the workforce during the pandemic.[163] These new associates have had limited in-person opportunities to observe norms and determine what is appropriate or effective within their organisations.[164] There may be a temptation to focus almost exclusively on these recent hires, but while special attention should be paid to this group, concentrating just on Gen Z will not adequately address the challenge.[165] The new hybrid era commands that organisations redefine professionalism for their entire workforce.[166]

Firms need to consider how their workplace norms have evolved and be explicit about them. Norms and behaviours are not just created in person; they are created remotely, and now we need to establish them

While there had been a decline in interest over recent years in pursuing partnership, a 2023 Major, Lindsey & Africa survey found that nearly 45% of associates said they would like to make partner at their firms.

in this new hybrid era. Again, it is the leaders and managers who need to set the example of what is acceptable and productive.

3.1 Millennial priorities

As we have mentioned, firms need to focus on establishing a work culture that attracts and retains their future leaders – Millennials. Lizzy McLellan, author of a seminal series of articles on Millennials in Big Law, noted that "millennials make up the largest generational group among lawyers at large and midsize firms" and that "the numbers starkly illustrate the reality facing law firm leaders: Millennials will soon take over the legal profession in sheer numbers – and soon enough they'll dominate leadership positions and partnerships, too".[167] Having a committed group of Millennials among a firm's partnership is critical for developing new client relationships and ensuring continued growth.[168]

While there had been a decline in interest over recent years in pursuing partnership, a 2023 Major, Lindsey & Africa survey found that nearly 45% of associates said they would like to make partner at their firms. This is a significant shift from the last survey in 2021, when 23.5% said they would like to make partner, and the two earlier surveys, in 2017 and 2019, which saw the number decrease from about 34% to 31%.[169]

Now that interest in becoming a partner has returned, firms need to capitalise on this and ensure that the path and end goal align with the needs and interests of their Millennials. Even pre-pandemic, when asked which benefits they would be willing to trade (regardless of tenure) the greatest percentage of partners favoured more time off.[170] After more time off, junior partners (which include the first Millennial partners) selected giving up cash compensation in exchange for a cut in billable hours, a flexible work schedule, better health benefits, more time for greater career planning and development, and more *pro bono* hours – in that order.[171] With Millennials' experience of remote work during the height of the pandemic, these preferences were only strengthened when people saw it was more possible than aspirational to live and work this way.

According to Michael Goldberg, general counsel for Simply Business, among Millennials "[t]here seems to be a greater appreciation for organizations that focus on empowerment and growth opportunities, have a clear mission or purpose, prioritize diversity and inclusion" and allow their employees "to be their authentic selves".[172] Millennials prioritise professional development and growth opportunities, including access to training workshops, programming and opportunities for advancement.[173] Moreover, they not only want formal development opportunities; they also seek leaders who take an interest in them and their development – they want guidance, direction, support and coaching.[174] With this cohort being the future of firms, it is worth taking note of their priorities.

3.2 Gen-learning styles

Firm leaders are also grappling with how to relate to a younger generation of associates that tend to appreciate clear, hands-on instruction rather than being left to their own devices, and still keep older generations engaged. Marcie Borgal Shunk recently asked a group of firm (Gen X) leaders about their challenges, and "multiple people shouted out 'Gen Z!'".[175] Gen X is a highly autonomous group of people.[176] "[F]or a group whose general attitude is 'figure it out,' there's a disconnect there."[177] However, this is not an impossible task. It just takes some thought as to how learning is best achieved. While implementing a one-size-fits-all training programme may seem most convenient and efficient for a law firm, taking the time to incorporate methods that serve a variety of learning and processing styles will better serve everyone in the long run.

(a) Boomers

Boomers are a highly educated generation that often learn best from proven experts. They seek out respected, high-profile institutions to further their education.[178] They also tend to be compliant learners and are still eager to learn. Most prefer in-person courses, but they have become more accustomed to online learning.[179]

(b) Gen X

Gen Xers tend to value independence and dislike micromanaging.[180] They prefer a more self-directed, practical learning plan. Gen Xers want to make sure the training is beneficial for their own development, and to know the learning goals and outcomes from the outset. They aren't afraid of technology, value learning that is easy and accessible, and appreciate being able to decide for themselves how and when they will learn.[181]

(c) Millennials

Millennials, many of whom grew up with social media, tend to be social learners.[182] They are proficient in hard skills and technical skills and expect technology to be part of the learning process. Millennials like to learn collaboratively and value feedback from a teacher. They also enjoy interactive microlearning and gamification.[183]

(d) Gen Z

Many Gen Zers, also known as Zoomers, have never known a life without digital technology.[184] They use TikTok or YouTube to learn and they prefer to learn independently, with bite-size content and microlearning. Gen Zers also want access on their mobile devices. They enjoy learning with others and welcome in-person activities.[185]

While implementing a one-size-fits-all training programme may seem most convenient and efficient for a law firm, taking the time to incorporate methods that serve a variety of learning and processing styles will better serve everyone in the long run.

3.3 Focus on happiness

There is no catch-all solution to retaining employees from all generations, but a firm's approach can be quite simple, according to Hasse Leonard-Pagel, consultant at Dilan Consulting Group.[186] Focus on what keeps people engaged and happy. For Gen Zers who have only experienced an uncertain legal market, it may be a solid development plan with a clear career path. For Gen X and Millennials, it may be maintaining workplace flexibility brought about by the pandemic. For Boomers, it may be acknowledging loyalty and recognising their expertise.[187]

For all, it is a mentally healthy, psychologically safe place to work. Actively listen to and create space for input from all levels of your workforce. Co-create your new norms while also rediscovering your firm traditions and celebrations. Find ways to intentionally bring people together to foster meaningful connections. A happy workforce makes for a productive workforce.

4. Change management

When looking at professional development programmes at a law firm, it helps to keep in mind that many newer associates, as Mark Masson, a partner and head of the professional services practice at Lotis Blue Consulting, has observed, "want to know where their career is going, the steps to get there".[188] They are focused on developing their own skills and often see their law firms as a means to an end. This "puts more onus on senior partners and [lawyers] to be more in-tune with how they're developing those lawyers".[189] Ample training opportunities, meaningful mentorship and attention to individualised growth are key to keeping this group engaged and motivated.

4.1 Feedback, feedback, feedback

Emphasis should be placed on more frequent in-the-moment feedback. And feedback can be done just as well remotely as in person. A healthy feedback culture – one in which senior lawyers and professional staff provide ongoing feedback to their teams as part of regular work practices – demonstrates to associates that their futures matter. This in turn produces better performance, greater team building, improved retention and stronger relationships.

(a) Encourage associates to ask

Firms should also focus on creating a culture in which asking for feedback is encouraged and expected. Junior lawyers should be given a sense of agency and responsibility for their professional development. According to the NeuroLeadership Institute, by creating the habit of asking for feedback we enable non-threatening and growth-oriented feedback conversations.[190] For the feedback giver,

Ongoing feedback is an essential component of leading differently and needs to be woven into the fabric of how a firm operates.

that means providing constructive, supportive feedback.[191] The receiver in turn accepts that feedback is an opportunity to grow, learn and improve.[192] Managers can foster this by sharing that they want to be asked and taking the time to model and ask: "How am I doing?"[193]

(b) Keep it casual

In addition to formal performance reviews (discussed below), ongoing informal feedback is crucial to lawyer growth and development. Lawyers constantly express their desire for more input from their managers, but accessing real-time feedback on a consistent basis with less face-to-face encounters can be challenging. Managers who take time to provide continual feedback, whether in person or remotely, create invaluable learning opportunities and help foster a stronger feedback culture at their firms.

It might help to be reminded that feedback does not take long. Send a quick email or schedule a five-minute debrief call with an associate, to share positive and constructive feedback.[194] Creating moments for virtual (or in-person) feedback sessions and checkpoints within workflows dedicated to reviewing performance are valuable tools to ensure frequent feedback. Ongoing feedback is an essential component of leading differently and needs to be woven into the fabric of how a firm operates. Managers need to make the effort and invest in regular feedback beyond the annual performance review.

(c) Equip direct managers

Creating the expectation that senior associates and counsel will also deliver feedback to more junior lawyers is another effective method of ensuring consistent and frequent feedback. Senior associates or counsel serve as important intermediaries, and when equipped with the right skills and information, can share the burden with supervising partners. Providing timely, consistent and transparent feedback affords associates the opportunity to course-correct in real time.[195]

4.2 Review upward (and all around)

A fundamental component of a strong feedback culture is creating a space where feedback flows upwards as well as downwards. Formal programmes such as upward reviews, which allow associates and professional staff to provide anonymous feedback about their managers, improve the performance of managers and offer newer associates and professional staff a meaningful voice in firm culture. 360° reviews, where feedback gathered from subordinates, colleagues and managers is combined with self-evaluation, represent another effective feedback tool allowing lawyers to get a holistic sense of their performance.

4.3 Don't neglect – or misuse – performance reviews

If your experience is that performance review season is met with some disdain in your office, you are not alone. Performance reviews are time consuming, labour intensive and potentially uncomfortable when constructive feedback is required. Some may even question whether they are really necessary. As Mark Masson notes:

> *It wasn't long ago where it was enough to know your work was good, and people said 'good job' once in a while, and you maybe got more pay, and you got on with it. That's not how it is anymore.*[196]

Time and effort given to conducting thorough and honest performance reviews is worth it. They provide the formal piece of the feedback puzzle and are critical for career development.

4.4 Make reviews positive and forward looking

Performance reviews are beneficial for both the law firm and lawyer. According to Michael S Cohen, partner at Duane Morris, they allow firms to acknowledge and celebrate successes, restate expectations, establish benchmarks for advancement and communicate any deficiencies in job performance.[197] The process may seem onerous for partners and senior lawyers, so providing proper training and formal guidance regarding how to draft meaningful evaluations is beneficial. It is equally – if not more – important to highlight the benefits of thoughtful reviews and the potential harms related to poorly drafted ones.[198]

The reviews should be approached through the lens of focusing on an employee's strengths, rather than emphasising his or her shortcomings. Diane Rosen, counsel at Ortoli Rosenstadt LLP, and Laurie Lyte, lawyer, coach and training professional, put it as follows:

> *Deficit-oriented performance reviews that emphasize what an employee is not doing well have been shown to fail to improve performance, and can be counterproductive, generating employee dissatisfaction and lower organizational performance.*[199]

It is no surprise that negative feedback focusing on mistakes and inadequacies is not especially motivating.[200] Emphasis should instead be placed on an affirmative, prospects-driven system that reinforces strengths and positive performance.[201] Gallup conducted several studies that show using a strengths-based approach to feedback increases engagement and productivity.[202]

We are not suggesting that law firms avoid negative feedback altogether, as it is important for lawyers to understand what didn't work. However, performance reviews should not be the first time a lawyer learns about an area that needs improvement. Constructive feedback needs to be given in the moment and then reinforced in the review.

A productive review should also include a fulsome discussion about a lawyer's future. Use the review as a moment for reflection with an eye toward where their career is heading. Associates want to know what opportunities lie ahead and what they can do to achieve their goals.

4.5 Don't skimp on reviews

It may be tempting to refrain from or skimp on performance reviews in a good year given the time-consuming nature of the process. However, cutting corners will cost a firm time and talent: time in terms of managing out weak performers who were not formally notified of their development needs, and talent in terms of the loss of good performers who might have benefitted from having their performance affirmed and supplemented with career development advice.

4.6 Consider doing reviews more often

Some firms used the pandemic as an opportunity to take a fresh look at their review processes and adjusted them to better suit their lawyers' needs. Paul Hastings started giving mid-year development-focused feedback, and informal reviews every few months.[203] Hogan Lovells eliminated its traditional system of annual performance reviews in 2018 and adopted its Pathways programme, in which associates ask partners about their performance throughout the year.[204] Reed Smith uses a mobile app for ongoing performance feedback from more senior lawyers.[205] Use whatever method works best for your firm and carve out the time more than once a year to ensure feedback is communicated to further bolster professional development and performance.

4.7 Performance lay-off cautions

Recently, an air of tension and angst among associates has been created by the sense that some law firms are conducting lay-offs under the guise of performance reviews.[206] Hijacking the review process for workforce reduction makes it hard to imagine reviews resulting in meaningful feedback and getting lawyers' attention to focus on their professional development.[207] There is the real chance that people hear the words, "You're safe", and shutdown to the rest of the review because they are relieved to have a job.[208] Performance management then becomes equated with ushering people out, rather than anticipated future planning between a partner and their subordinate. This creates a culture of distrust and apprehension, and signals to the workforce that their development is not a priority.

4.8 Formal training continues

Maintaining formal training programmes was a vital aspect of supporting lawyers throughout the pandemic. Successful firms substantially augmented their existing programmes with training targeted at the challenges of remote work and finding effective ways to conduct remote training. Remote training tools are cost effective and efficient and should continue to be an integral part of a firm's training platform.

Training strategies for hybrid working

Firms should add hybrid work-specific topics and should consider starting (or continuing) to shift their standard training approaches to better fit hybrid learning needs. Successful strategies might include:

- rolling out a range of learning modes tailored for in-person and remote experiences;
- coordinating in-office schedules to match training opportunities;
- augmenting internal training resources;
- reducing the length of training to more bite-sized durations; and
- making the programmes themselves highly engaging and collaborative.

4.9 Addressing the talent gap

As we know, the pandemic forced Gen Z to miss out on vital experiences as they spent almost two years of high school, college or law school stuck at home.[209] They missed out on the hands-on experience of internships and first jobs, but they still had to go to work.[210]

Establishing the percentage of lawyers and professional staff who joined during the pandemic and considering the intentional interventions they need is important. Rather than bemoaning what those joiners are missing due to a lack of in-person interactions, identify their development needs and create programmes that specifically address those deficiencies. It's not too late.

If you have internal benchmarks, you may want to simplify and refresh them, and assess this new cohort against these. Ask group leaders what they are seeing. Then ask, What assignments are needed to solve for this? Is it business skills, executive presence, client interaction, email etiquette? Get granular and figure out who can get the cohort this exposure. The talent gap does not need to be viewed as calamitous. This is fixable. Ideally, do not wait for performance reviews to evaluate these deficiencies, but consider reviews your stop gap and use them as opportunities to look for trends in terms of needs. Have methods in place to identify support needs as they arise.

Remote training tools are cost effective and efficient and should continue to be an integral part of a firm's training platform.

Several of the large US accounting firms now offer specialised training for Gen Z workers, including special classes on soft skills for incoming hires.[211] The classes include training in teamwork, giving presentations and face-to-face communication. In short, they cover "everything that people (used to) learn by osmosis during the earliest stages of their career".[212] This is just one way to address potential skills gaps among new hires. Tailored assignments, one-on-one coaching and mentorship exercises are some other ways to provide this instruction.

4.10 Ready to launch

Another professional development tool often used by other industries like consulting is the launch meeting. Scott Westfahl, professor of practice and director of executive education at Harvard Law School, shared with *Law360* that lawyer teams "rarely hold a launch meeting when a project starts, even though research shows team launches highly correlate with team success".[213] These meetings help the project's mission to come alive for people.[214] Westfahl notes:

> *Meaning and purpose abound in projects and in partners' personal stories about why they love their work. Yet associates rarely hear about any of that, especially at the project ... level.*[215]

Sharing why a project matters, who the client is, how the firm is trying to help and the nature of each team member's role on the project will

Including the entire team in the how and why sets the tone for a collaborative project, where everyone's contribution is valued and important. Often, for associates and professional staff, it is easy to get lost in the weeds working on discrete portions of a larger matter. The launch meeting helps connect the dots at the outset.

help build team morale, engagement and motivation.[216] Including the entire team in the how and why sets the tone for a collaborative project, where everyone's contribution is valued and important. Often, for associates and professional staff, it is easy to get lost in the weeds working on discrete portions of a larger matter. The launch meeting helps connect the dots at the outset.

4.11 Tell your clients what you're doing

As economic pressures continue, AI becomes more prevalent, and the impacts of remote work on professional development unfold, some clients may start to question the value – and rates – of associates assigned to their projects.[217] Not only is it essential that firms place a significant focus on training and professional development; they should not hesitate to share with clients the steps they are taking and the resources they are investing to correct for any learning loss.[218] Also consider that many clients may be struggling with the same training gaps in their legal departments, so invite them to join you and be a part of your professional development programming – plan trainings together, collaborate on CLEs and share best practices.

4.12 Keep mentoring, and mentoring, and mentoring

One of the most powerful forms of professional development is mentoring. Whether through formal firm programmes or informal relationships, one-on-one connections between senior lawyers and those more junior are critically important to both individual lawyer development and a sense of cohesive firm culture. According to Hasse Leonard-Pagel, consultant at Dilan Consulting Group, "younger employees benefit from the wisdom and skills of their older peers while offering older employees a valuable new perspective of their own".[219] As relationships are built (and rebuilt) with a return (at least on some days) by many lawyers to the office, focus should be placed on bolstering formal mentorship programmes while the informal relationships catch up.

(a) Formal mentoring

Formal mentoring programmes, which match associates with more senior lawyers (typically partners) whose practice areas align with their career goals, are a hallmark of law firms that aim to promote a strong learning culture. These programmes are also crucial to ensuring that associates who do not develop an organic informal mentoring relationship are not left behind in their development. Strategies that can help support strong mentoring programmes include:

- proactively reaching out to both lawyers and professional staff to solicit participation;
- following up with participants to ensure they have adequate resources to support their communications and provide ideas to keep the conversations ongoing;

- circulating tip sheets to remind participants about valuable online communication tools; and
- identifying lawyers who need particular support and ensuring they have upstream assistance to address their unique challenges.

(b) Informal mentoring

While formal mentoring has an important place in ensuring that every junior associate receives access to a mentor, the mentoring relationships that develop naturally can often be stronger than those that are assigned. With both associates and more senior lawyers in the office less frequently, there is less in-person opportunity for these natural relationships to form. Adding to the challenge, as Paul Schmidt explains, is that senior associates and young partners are often "the best mentors for new lawyers and drive enthusiasm for the job because they have relevant experience, but they also tend to have the most going on outside of work".[220] They are the people who benefit the most from the flexibility.[221] Keep in mind that associates may hesitate to initiate these connections, so as not to seem bothersome. Thus, it is crucial that partners and senior associates appear – and are – receptive to forming these bonds.

Intentionality is crucial to reinvigorating the bonds that form between newer lawyers and their managers. Creating both in-person and digital opportunities for connection will ensure that informal mentoring does not get lost in this new era. When firms emphasise relationship building and demonstrate a commitment to developing the workforce, mentoring becomes a natural part of their ethos.

4.13 Build skills

(a) Stay committed to pro bono

Demand for *pro bono* legal service is as high as ever, and there is a dearth of volunteers for most programmes.[222] Of course there are altruistic reasons to work on *pro bono* matters, but these projects also provide substantive opportunities for developing talent. Lawyers build skill sets, expand their networks, work collaboratively with colleagues and cultivate their professional interests. *Pro bono* work also fosters connection and relationship building among colleagues through a shared commitment to helping others – both central elements of a thriving firm culture. Moreover, *pro bono* work helps lawyers rediscover their commitment to practising law and acts as a reminder that the intention of practising law is to help others.[223]

(b) Hybrid business development

Successful firms ensure that business development is part of the fabric of each lawyer's training, in ways appropriate to their seniority.

During the pandemic, the shifting market necessitated changes to firm strategies and training regarding business development. Many common engagements like conferences, lunches and client visits were not an option. Firms had to get creative, and many approaches proved to be very effective. Several are still valuable in the hybrid era.

Business development in the hybrid era

We suggest incorporating some of the following approaches in today's business development training efforts:

- Understand how the client prefers to work – remotely or in person.
- Anticipate client needs as the market shifts and then proactively reach out to offer advice and engage in discovery discussions to learn more about new ways to support clients.
- Continue to leverage online presence, by continually updating online profiles with representative matters and niche expertise, pushing out new content and connecting with new contacts.[224]
- Collaborate with colleagues to cross-sell services, especially in emerging areas.
- Develop an awareness of fee structures and sensitivity to billing issues.
- Offer in-person and virtual options to reach a larger audience.
- Explore virtual communication tools that provide face time, which can be more effective than traditional phone calls for certain settings.[225]

These tools raise visibility, help keep lawyers top of mind for clients, and foster relationship building.

The pandemic also brought about a heightened awareness of the importance of cutting-edge technologies to stay connected, assess markets, streamline aspects of legal practice and track marketing and sales efforts. Training lawyers on the benefits and use of these new technologies, including AI, will be crucial to cultivating a modernised practice.

4.14 Summer programme evolution

Summer programmes are an opportunity to showcase the culture and unique personality of a firm and help foster a sense of community and pride for the entire office. The hybrid era brings yet another evolution in the summer associate programme and it should reflect the changed nature of law firm life. Many firms are having their summer associates follow a hybrid schedule, similar to their full-time counterparts.[226] Brittney Padilla, attorney recruiting manager at Ogletree Deakins, explained in a *Thomson Reuters* post that "[w]hile in-person interaction is very important, summers also benefit from doing business virtually, which is much more commonplace today".[227] Firms are also making a concerted effort to encourage summer associates to foster connections and a sense of community across their entire firm, not just a local office, using virtual tools and hosting virtual events.[228] This mirrors the new reality of much more integrated firm operations. Of course, strong mentorship programmes and training opportunities continue to be a must, and again should emulate the more evolved approaches offered to the entire office.

4.15 People management

Performance management and how it is implemented reveals a lot about a firm's culture. It signals to a workforce whether their professional development is truly a priority for the firm. Again, clear communication and authenticity are key components of effective and well-received performance management practices.

4.16 Holding back

As an alternative to lay-offs, some law firms are taking advantage of the shift to an employer-driven market by making more subtle adjustments to their associate workforce.[229] Recently, legal recruiters in California and New York have reported an abnormal number of associates being asked to take a class year reduction or being told they won't advance with the rest of their class.[230] If law firms opt to use these methods, delivery of the information is critical and transparency is key. If the hold-back is for performance reasons, state that. If it is for larger economic ones, communicate that as well. Reinforcing an associate's strengths and the long-term benefits of the decision will help the information land on receptive ears.

4.17 Confidential in-house coaching

In-house career coaching programmes are beneficial for lawyers remaining at a firm who are navigating unforeseen changes to their career trajectories. Professional development departments can offer one-on-one coaching to address individual issues such as a reduction in work for certain practice areas, lawyers' desire to pivot to new practice areas, and planning progress towards professional goals and milestones. The coaching can be especially beneficial for lawyers who are struggling with performance issues or trying to scope out long-term career plans.

4.18 Soft landing for exits

When circumstances (whether performance- or finance-based) require that an individual exit a firm, management of the process is important for morale. Prioritising career advising and *alumni* support programmes reinforces a firm culture that is people focused and demonstrates a firm's commitment to supporting the entire arc of an individual's career. Law firms that offer career transition support, facilitate placement with clients, arrange secondments and provide outplacement consulting programmes to help lawyers who are laid off, foster a lasting bond and demonstrate a sense of appreciation for the careers of these lawyers beyond the firm.

4.19 Key takeaways

A strong commitment to developing your people is essential to a thriving firm culture. Focus on:

- creating an environment where questions and feedback flow freely, remotely and in person;
- embracing the new hybrid norm and making in-office time meaningful;
- focusing on your Millennials;
- recognising learning preferences and offering a variety of learning options;
- incorporating feedback as a frequent and encouraged practice;
- providing meaningful performance reviews;
- addressing (not bemoaning) the talent gap; and
- prioritising mentor relationships.

IV. Well-being and flexibility

1. What it is and why it matters

Lawyers are struggling with mental health and substance abuse, and are burning out at alarming rates.[231] Unsurprisingly, a recent analysis by *The Washington Post* identified law as being the most stressful profession.[232] And the stats continue to show a decline in mental health. In ALM's annual Mental Health Survey from 2023, 71.1% of lawyers said they had anxiety and 38.2% said they were depressed, both figures up from 2022.[233] The number of lawyers who said they had an additional mental health issue more than doubled to 31.2% in 2023, from 14.6% in 2022.[234] And this is not just a Big Law problem. "[L]awyers at midsize firms have almost all the same mental health struggles as their Big Law compatriots."[235] In-house lawyers are struggling too.[236]

People from marginalised identity groups face disproportionate challenges around mental health and work. In a Mind Share Partners and Qualtrics study from 2023, women, Gen Z, Black, Latinx and LGBTQ+ respondents all tended to have worse mental health outcomes than their counterparts and were less likely to get a supportive response when they talked about their mental health at work.[237]

Layer on healing from pandemic trauma and lawyers are grappling with a lot, both physically and mentally.[238] Instead of the stress being of the moment, the pandemic created an environment where stress was constant – where, according to Dr Larry Richard, it "[wore] out the circuit".[239] What's more worrisome is that lawyers aren't feeling any more comfortable using mental health and substance abuse resources, extended-leave policies, or onsite wellness professionals.[240]

Given the precarious state of the overall well-being of lawyers today, it is essential that law firms prioritise the mental health of their workforce. There are organisational benefits for investing in wellness as well. Focusing on lawyer and professional staff well-being can reduce healthcare spending and positively affect other metrics like absence and attrition rates, billable hours and employee engagement.[241]

It is also wise for law firms to pursue strategies and interventions aimed at improving flexibility, so that lawyers and professional staff can "thrive across all dimensions of their lives".[242] Firms that grasp the increased need for support for wellness and flexibility will enhance their firm culture and signal to their employees that they care about their workforce.

Firms that grasp the increased need for support for wellness and flexibility will enhance their firm culture and signal to their employees that they care about their workforce.

2. Considerations in a hybrid work environment

There are two separate conversations to be had when considering hybrid work and its impact on lawyer well-being:

- return-to-office policies; and
- the wellness considerations of flexible work arrangements and in-person interactions.

Both conversations play critical roles in the well-being space.

2.1 Return to the office

Return-to-office policies have become an outlier in an environment where Big Law firms typically follow in lockstep what their counterparts are doing. Firms are making their own decisions in terms of what works for their business, rather than falling in line with everyone else.[243] Though firms are taking several different approaches, most have created some sort of plan related to in-office time. A Saville's Law Firm Return-to-Office survey conducted in May 2023, in which around 70 US firms participated, found that 90% have implemented a policy regarding in-office attendance, with 50% recommending some level of attendance and 34% requiring it.[244]

The survey also found that 62% of larger firms with more than 250 lawyers mandate or recommend in-office attendance three days a week, while half of smaller firms follow the same schedule.[245] Only 16% of larger firms and 10% of smaller firms recommend or mandate attendance twice a week. About a quarter of the smaller firms have no in-office attendance policy.[246]

Several big Wall Street firms have mandated returns to the office, requiring four-day attendance as of September 2023. Weil, Skadden and Davis Polk are some of the names on that list.[247] Ropes & Gray mandated four days in November 2023, the new schedule also applying to associates in the firm's London and Dublin offices.[248] Their Asia offices have returned to a pre-pandemic schedule of five days a week in the office.[249] These firms appear to be capitalising on a slowdown in demand and a cooling talent market, which has put more control back in the hands of law firm leaders to dictate work schedules.[250]

However, a number of large West Coast firms aren't following their East Coast peers.[251] DLA Piper has called its approach a "high-performance flexibility" model that combines remote and in-office work with no hard requirements.[252] Proponents of this approach say it is helping recruit and retain top talent, including increasing their talent pool and expanding their roster of lawyers beyond their geographic boundaries.[253] They also say it better supports lawyers whose life circumstances necessitate a flexible arrangement.[254]

Southeast law firms are "forging their own paths" with policies that combine flexibility for more senior lawyers and some level of in-office training for new associates.[255]

Yet another approach is letting practice groups, offices and individual lawyers dictate their work pattern.[256] Spencer Fane is experimenting with this bottom-up approach. Firm chair Pat Whalen considers that allowing his workforce extra autonomy on where they work is driving better engagement.[257] This approach allows groups and individuals to decide what best suits their – and their clients' – needs, rather than forcing the entire firm to follow one set schedule.

In the United Kingdom, office attendance policies vary as in the United States. Antonia Klein, a director and co-owner of Law Absolute, told *Law360* that the "general trend in London is that law firms are wanting people back in the office more than they work at home".[258] There is a real push for office attendance, with an expectation of at least three days a week.[259] For many firms, this is to align with the transactional needs of banking and finance clients, who have been eager to get back into the office.[260] Osborne Clarke recently announced that it expects lawyers and professional staff to spend at least three days a week in its offices and will consider attendance when evaluating performance bonuses.[261] Employees typically still prefer to work flexibly, but there is increasingly less opportunity to do so. And US law firms have been "the driving force" behind getting people back into the office in London, according to Jason Connolly, founder and chief executive of legal recruitment firm JMC Legal.[262] Other firms, such as Kingsley Napley and Dentons, have maintained flexible work arrangements and have reduced office space as a result.[263]

Global law firms are also grappling with whether to apply a one-size-fits-all approach to all their offices.[264] This is proving more difficult than expected, as their offices "straddle multiple cultures, all home to differing expectations for how work gets done".[265] Some firms have chosen a consistent mandate that applies equally across offices, while others have set varying standards for office attendance, taking into account cultural expectations, hiring-market dynamics and client practices in each region.[266] For example, Wilmer Cutler – which has offices in London, the United States, Brussels, Berlin, Frankfurt and Beijing – expects all of its lawyers to be in the office three days a week.[267] The Dutch firm, De Brauw Blackstone Westbroek, says its current policy is that any employee is expected to work half of their working days a week at the office.[268] The firm has offices in Singapore, Shanghai, London, Brussels and Amsterdam.[269] On the other hand, lawyers at Quinn Emanuel's London office are generally required to come into the office three days a week, while their counterparts in the firm's US offices follow a work-from-anywhere policy.[270]

Jeffrey Lowe of Major, Lindsey & Africa predicts that as office attendance policies continue to evolve they have "the potential to become a very significant differentiator over the next couple of years, depending upon which road the different firms go in terms of mandating office return", adding that in-office policies may be "one of the more important issues if not the most important issue" for law firm management over the next several years.[271]

What approach should your firm take? The West Coast, Southeast and 'bottom-up' approaches better align with lawyer preferences. According to *The American Lawyer* survey data, the "strong majority of lawyers want some form of remote work".[272] The policy you choose also says something about a firm's culture. This is a lot about trust and the approach a firm takes sends a strong signal to its workforce about the environment it seeks to create.

2.2 Associate frustration

While firms navigate how to approach office policies, "a growing number of associates are taking issue with not just new attendance policies, but how firms communicate and deploy their return-to-work strategies".[273] They are frustrated with the lack of clear guidance, transparency or an opportunity to offer input.[274] It is imperative that firms alleviate this frustration by offering clear and consistent policy standards and creating channels for associate feedback.

2.3 The policing challenge

One of the complications of return-to-office mandates is policing. Cox, Castle & Nicholson managing partner Dwayne McKenzie comments as follows:

> *[E]mployees often find ways around office mandates ... If you aren't policing it, there doesn't seem to be much point, and [i]f you are policing it, that's going to have an effect on your environment.*[275]

Policing return-to-office mandates requires monitoring and enforcement, which can create an adversarial, distrustful atmosphere.

Lawyers may also find the policing somewhat degrading and counterproductive. According to Sanford Michelman, chairman and co-founder of California midsize firm Michelman & Robinson, "culturally, it'll get worse if you treat people like widgets".[276] This is especially the case when lawyers are already "constantly scrutinising their investment of time for what's billable".[277] The hour spent getting to and from the office is often viewed as an hour lost for billing.[278] When a lawyer is stripped of the ability to decide whether the commuting time is worth it for the day, the frustration may only intensify.

2.4 Bonus jeopardy

If the chatter continues that some firms will now tie office attendance to bonus eligibility, be prepared for law firm culture to take a hit. Davis Polk told employees in 2023 that their bonuses could be cut if they don't work from the company's office at least three days per week.[279] Several other Big Law firms have issued similar announcements.[280] The policing required to implement these policies removes a valued sense of trust and autonomy that helps build firm culture. It also compounds the stress from existing billable requirements to include an attendance requirement as well.[281] This is in direct tension with what newer lawyers say they want from their law firms, which is increased flexibility and a healthier balance between their professional and personal lives.[282] Decreases in bonuses or a change in bonus structure send a strong message about what is valued, can greatly impact morale and should be approached with care, equity and transparency. Don't forget that law firms had some of their most productive and profitable years during the height of the pandemic.[283] Lawyers worked from home, were paid extra money, and it worked.

2.5 The well-being case for flexibility

From a mental health perspective, flexibility is a key component of well-being as law firms redefine their workplace structures.[284] When employees have more control over their schedules and work arrangements, they can better manage their stress levels and avoid burnout.[285] Notably, women and BIPOC (Black, indigenous and people of colour) are more likely than white males to prefer remote work.[286] As Amy Johnston, clinical director at Urban Wellness and co-creator of the All-Rise Initiative, explains, "Leaders who do not identify with a marginalized group may not understand all of the factors which contribute to someone's preference for working remotely," such as the prevalence of micro- and macro-aggressions in their work space.[287] It is critical for leaders to be thoughtful in their approach to demonstrate support for their entire workforce and the unique circumstances each individual may face.[288] Firms that offer flexible work options signal to their workforce that they matter as individuals and that they trust their employees to do their best work in the environment that suits them best. This fosters a culture of respect and demonstrates that your firm values real contribution over face time and when or where work gets done.[289]

Interestingly, according to Gallup's 2023 Global State of the Workplace Report, employed individuals who were working remotely either full-time or part-time said they were experiencing more stress and more anger than employees who were working onsite full-time.[290] At the same time, data showed that "remote and hybrid employees across the world were consistently more engaged than onsite employees, which correlates with higher productivity and performance".[291] While

If the chatter continues that some firms will now tie office attendance to bonus eligibility, be prepared for law firm culture to take a hit.

not focused on the unique environment of a law firm setting, this research may further support the need for employee flexibility and autonomy to decide the work environment (hybrid or in-person) that best supports the needs of the workforce and their potential for maximum performance.

2.6 The well-being case for coming in

While it is clear that most lawyers favour flexibility and autonomy, Patrick Krill, a lawyer and thought leader in the well-being space, cautions that "[t]here are real and tangible risks and downsides to working from home on a protracted basis".[292] Mental health and substance use problems are more likely to grow if someone is regularly isolated or only required to be around colleagues a few times a week. Moreover, when people are not observed on a regular basis, these problems can be much more difficult to detect.[293]

Being on the lookout for the following signs may help identify a problem:

- changes in communication patterns, including inconsistencies in an employee's communications such as long lags, delays;
- changes in physical presentation, appearing unkempt, tired or even dishevelled;

- changes in mood, regularly seeming distracted, on edge or irritable;
- cancellations, tardiness, forgetfulness; and
- overproductivity, working long days or unusual hours (while it may seem paradoxical, being overproductive may be a warning sign of emotional or mental health issues – an effort by employees to avoid their feelings).[294]

Increased attention and meaningful time spent with colleagues will be crucial to providing healthy human interaction and identifying those who may be struggling.

In addition, certain career development experiences for lawyers have to be done in person. Career success is fundamental to well-being.

3. Generational considerations
The generational strife in the workplace spills over into wellness conversations as well. In fact, it is an area of heightened concern for younger generations and can seem out of place for some in the older generations. More experienced lawyers feel like they are in a service industry where client demands come first, and their younger counterparts are pushing back on that notion.[295]

Increased attention and meaningful time spent with colleagues will be crucial to providing healthy human interaction and identifying those who may be struggling.

3.1 Gen Z values

Gen Z places an extremely high value on flexibility – a trend, according to Jacqueline Bokser LeFebvre, managing director and co-author of a recent survey conducted by Major, Lindsey & Africa, that has been heightened by the pandemic.[296] "Sixty-two per cent of respondents said they would trade a portion of their compensation for more time off, 60% for a flexible work schedule ... and 41% for reduction in billable hours."[297] A recent Williams Lea (a support services provider for professional firms) report noted that "any perceived lack of flexibility will turn off Gen Z" employees.[298] The new generation of lawyers "wants flexibility and to be treated as adults. They will be there when they're needed, but they don't want to be forced into the office every day".[299] Given Gen Z's preferences, it is not surprising that "[t]ension is growing between associates and partners along fault lines of hourly commitments and return-to-office policies".[300] Associates continue to ask for more flexibility and lower billable-hour requirements, while some partners believe this generation's expectations are incompatible with the realities of a profession that is supposed to hold client service above all else.[301]

Whether Boomers and Gen Xers continue to disagree with Gen Z and their "raised expectations of what a 'healthy' workplace should look like," Gen Z is here to stay.[302] Gen Zers are also "giving more serious consideration to career paths that might pay less, but offer other benefits like flexible and remote work, part-time work policies and mental health services and support".[303] Rather than disregard their value-driven approach as youthful naivety, it will be beneficial for employers to understand and appreciate their priorities.[304] Otherwise, law firms may find themselves struggling to not only get this next generation in the door, but to convince them to stay.

3.2 Finding common ground (and support)

Though each generation may view the legal profession through a different lens, common ground exists on how to support a multigenerational workforce:

- Emphasise professional growth and development among employees of all ages, including those 50 and older.
- Offer flexible work arrangements, allowing employees to maintain their employment, job performance and productivity when navigating life phases such as starting a family, caregiving, going back to school or transitioning into retirement.
- Support caregiving employees – this is a responsibility shared across generations.
- Offer flexible retirement options, enabling valuable lawyers to stay on who seek to transition but are not ready to fully retire.
- Provide comprehensive health, welfare and retirement benefits.[305]

In an industry whose culture is often considered high stress, firms willing to embrace changing norms and prioritise well-being and flexibility will elevate their cultures and lay the groundwork for improved wellness, improved productivity and improved outcomes for clients. It is important for this shift to start at the top.

4. Change management

In an industry whose culture is often considered high stress, firms willing to embrace changing norms and prioritise well-being and flexibility will elevate their cultures and lay the groundwork for improved wellness, improved productivity and improved outcomes for clients. It is important for this shift to start at the top. Leaders who prioritise well-being, promote a culture of openness and acceptance and normalise seeking help will help foster a healthy, productive and successful work environment.

4.1 Importance of psychosocial safety

'Psychosocial safety' may be a less familiar term for some than 'psychological safety' (referred to above), but its introduction is helpful as a framework for leaders who are committed to cultivating a safe and positive work culture and improving employee well-being.[306] Whereas psychological safety refers to a work environment where individuals feel safe to express ideas and admit mistakes without fear of repercussions, psychosocial safety is broader in scope.

Psychosocial hazards arise from "aspects of work design, the work itself, and the interactions between employees which can negatively influence their mental health and emotional wellbeing".[307] Examples of psychosocial hazards that may cause psychological and physical harm can arise from or relate to:

- the design or management of work including job demands and job design;
- the physical working environment;
- rewards and recognition;
- workplace interactions or behaviours;[308] and
- poor change management.

These hazards are things at work that create stress.[309] Creating psychosocial safety is a management approach that prioritises organisational policies, procedures and practices to protect employees' psychological well-being.[310]

Currently, many lawyers don't feel that their firms have created a safe environment. In *The American Lawyer*'s 2023 survey of mental health in the legal profession, when asked about the sources of their mental health struggles lawyers blamed their firms and the nature of the legal profession.[311] More than three-quarters said their work environment contributed to their mental health issues, and the top reasons selected as to why firms adversely affected lawyers' mental health were billable-hour pressures, always being on call, lack of sleep and client demands.[312] Some law firm cultures can also add expectations of perfection and fears of humiliation over mistakes, both of which keep lawyers in a constant state of apprehension and tension.[313]

Firm policies and procedures and the work environment firm leaders create directly impact the well-being of lawyers and professional staff. Ensuring that psychosocial safety is considered at each step of the decision-making process will help foster a safe and productive work environment.

Ways to promote psychosocial safety (which also align with positive culture building) include:

- creating a positive and supportive culture;
- prioritising training and onboarding;
- fostering supportive leadership through training;
- constructing strong lines of communication;
- facilitating career development; and
- providing managers with psychosocial safety training.[314]

4.2 Remove the stigma

One often-cited reason that lawyers do not seek mental health care or support until it is too late is stigma.[315] According to McKinsey experts Erica Coe, Jenny Cordina, Kana Enomoto and Nikhil Seshan: "In behavioral health, 'stigma' is defined as a level of shame, prejudice, or discrimination toward people with mental-health or substance-use conditions."[316] There is a real fear of being judged as inadequate, lesser, or a failure and that career aspirations will be limited by admitting the need for help.[317] Many therefore stay silent about their struggles and pretend that nothing is wrong, at a time when people are most vulnerable and in need of help.[318] As noted by the same experts: "This terrible paradox can deepen an illness that is often invisible to others."[319]

4.3 We've seen some improvement, but not enough

There has been some progress in terms of openness about mental health in the workplace. Among British workers, 32% felt more comfortable talking about their mental health in the workplace in 2022, compared to 14% in mid-2019.[320] The United States experienced similar progress: some 51% of workers were comfortable talking openly about mental health at work in April 2019, increasing to 65% in September 2019.[321] However, workers continue to be concerned about workplace judgement when it comes to mental health. McKinsey research from 2021 showed that more than half of survey respondents feared stigma if co-workers discovered their mental health problems.[322] June 2022 data from LifeWorks found that 91% of Britons, 92% of Americans and 90% of Australians believe that people with mental health conditions are treated differently, which is known to discourage individuals from seeking support and treatment in the workplace.[323]

Table 4: What best describes the level of stigma in your workplace?[324]

Stigma levels	Don't know	High-level	Some-to-moderate	Little	None
Mental illness	6%	18%	52%	16%	8%
Substance use disorder	6%	20%	49%	18%	7%

4.4 Costs and benefits

Not only can mental health care transform the lives of employees and their loved ones, there is a significant business case for reducing stigma and improving access to mental health support as well.[325] Employees and their dependents with mental health conditions make up a large proportion of employers' healthcare spending. Moreover, "The World Health Organization estimates that lost productivity due to depression and anxiety alone costs the global economy $1 trillion annually."[326] Mental health disorders are also a primary cause of worker disability. And treatment works: over 80% of employees who receive mental health care say they become more effective and satisfied at work.[327]

4.5 Steps to removal

For law firms that are committed to dismantling stigma, the most effective strategy is top-down modelling from leadership.[328] If firm leaders have mental health struggles of their own, opening up about them can be a great starting point:[329]

> *Leaders who are able to be authentic and transparent, share their struggles, and model mentally healthy behaviors create a culture of connection, support and flexibility.*[330]

Lawyers and professional staff will feel comfortable telling others what they are going through and seek the help they need, if they see those in leadership positions doing the same.[331]

Seeing leaders open up will also demonstrate to more junior lawyers that having a mental health issue is not detrimental to their careers.[332] Lawyers and professional staff need to see that they won't be penalised – even reputationally – by seeking help.[333] If role models in leadership positions aren't visible, the profession implicitly conveys that success and mental health support are mutually exclusive.[334]

To that end, it is important that law firms devote time and space to regular discussions around mental health in the workplace. Dr Kendall Browne of Lyra Health recommends an all-firm approach:

> *Company-wide training can help teams notice and respond appropriately to signs of psychological distress in themselves and those around them, develop strategies to reduce stigma in mental health, and get connected to resources that can support their mental health and well-being.*[335]

However, progress is not only made through formal programming. According to Amy Johnston: "Every time a person in power asks others how they are doing and genuinely listens to their concerns, they dismantle stigma."[336] When leaders communicate and model that prioritising mental health is not only acceptable, but beneficial, for success, they are creating a safe space for their workforce to do the same.[337] In addition, providing a comprehensive mental health resource that makes it easy for employees to access care demonstrates that your firm is invested in making a tangible difference in employees' health and well-being.[338]

4.6 Elevate all voices

It is important that all members of a law firm feel seen, heard and supported, especially marginalised groups. This is key to psychological safety:

> *When we layer on the social injustices, incidents of violence and political upheaval of the past few years, it is understandable that symptoms of anxiety and hypervigilance are flaring, especially for BIPOC, Asian Americans and Pacific Islanders, members of the lesbian, gay, bisexual, transgender and queer (LGBTQ+) community, [certain religious groups,] and other marginalised populations.*[339]

Any conversation about psychological health, safety and well-being in the workplace must consider diversity and inclusion as a core element.[340] Thoughtful consideration of which employee experiences are recognised and given attention, and which may be left out, can help design solutions that support the populations who are affected most broadly and create a sense of belonging for everyone at the firm.[341] It is imperative that leaders genuinely take the time to listen and create a safe space for dialogue to ensure that all voices are heard and everyone's experiences are recognised.

4.7 Train and support managers

Firms can support their partners and others who fill management roles by providing mental health awareness training, including guidance on helping a struggling co-worker appropriately.[342] Managers should be

It is important that all members of a law firm feel seen, heard and supported, especially marginalised groups.

equipped to help employees by reducing barriers to seeking support, navigating any needed time away from work, and accommodating and supporting a successful return to the workplace.[343] Providing support for the individual mental health needs of managers is also critical.[344] Managers carry the emotional responsibility of their subordinates, but individually may not be prepared to manage their own mental health needs, model behaviours, or serve as a resource.[345]

4.8 Be creative in your delivery

Patrick Krill has this advice:

> *The firms that have had the most success in building a well-being program that their lawyers and professional staff appreciate and take seriously are firms that recognize – as an organizing principle – that a one size-fits-all approach is bound for mediocrity.*[346]

Delivering programming and resources through multiple formats (live, on-demand, app-based, video, podcast and print) ensures that it reaches the widest audience, is available when needed, and is suitable for several learning styles.[347] And whatever medium is used, ensure that the programming is authentic and true to your culture and values.

4.9 Bring on resources and staff

Bringing resources and practitioners in-house to assist with well-being and mental health needs is another way to ensure that lawyers and professional staff have direct and convenient access to the support they need.[348] It removes the extra layer of finding outside support and navigating insurance, and eliminates the often long lead times in securing appointments with mental health professionals. George Demos, a healthcare partner and chief operating officer at O'Melveny, has described how the firm hired its first director of well-being, Nora Minno, who is a registered dietitian, certified personal trainer and behavioural specialist.[349] Dedicating the resources to creating these positions signals that firm leaders are committed to the well-being of those at the firm and makes the use of these resources more accepted and accessible.[350]

4.10 The billable dilemma

While internal well-being positions, robust mental health resources and support from firm management are all crucial to creating a thriving workforce and healthy culture, the elephant in the room remains the billable hour. Lawyers "across firm sizes ranked the billable hour highest among all other law firm stressors in terms of its negative impact on their mental health".[351] Compounding this stressor

While internal well-being positions, robust mental health resources and support from firm management are all crucial to creating a thriving workforce and healthy culture, the elephant in the room remains the billable hour.

at Big Law is that with billing rates set so high, some lawyers feel that a normal person can't work at the intensity to justify the cost, and thus only bill an hour for what can be 1.5 to 2 hours of work.[352]

One option considered by some firms is offering alternative tracks that involve a lower billable hours requirement, which can range from 1,600 hours to as low as 1,000 hours.[353] Being supportive of flexible hour arrangements provides lawyers with more control over their schedules and the ability to obtain a greater balance in their lives.[354]

Reducing billable targets for all lawyers to 1,800 hours is another idea being floated and is supported by two state bar associations.[355] It was the typical amount many large firms used to require until the tech boom of the 1990s.[356] It is also "the maximum amount of work most people can do without hurting their physical or mental health, according to scientific research".[357] However, there appears to be little movement from Big Law to consider any reductions and doing so would cut into the bottom line.[358]

Communication and training regarding billing may also alleviate some of the angst surrounding billable hours. Some firms don't offer formalised training programmes to help lawyers understand the importance of billing at a high level for the firm's economic survival, or offer a standardised process for how to bill, according to Kristen Corpian, a former Greenberg Traurig associate and now a partner and the chief innovation officer at Trembly Law:[359]

> *Ultimately, if you don't understand a process, why it's important, and how to do it right – however your company defines 'right' – then you are just left to swing and miss, which leaves [lawyers] feeling uncertain and angry at the process overall.*[360]

Clear expectations, standards and processes for billing ensure that all lawyers are operating under the same set of principles.

Other ways to combat billing stress include evening hard-stops on internal emails and new work assignments, and formalised no-contact rules for vacations.[361] These steps create space for meaningful breaks and time to rest and recover.

Ultimately, it's not the billable hour itself that is the problem. It's what it represents – the badges of honour that are associated with it. It's how the billable hour gets done and how people are supported as they work it.

At the end of the billable year, be sure that your review process offers lawyers the opportunity to present a full picture of where their time is going, and the meaningful contributions made beyond what their hours reflect – and reward these efforts.

4.11 Work–life hanging in the balance

When creating (and revising) workplace policies, a crucial question to ask is: "[H]ow will this promote much-needed balance for hardworking employees?"[362] Hybrid flexibility helps, but significant attention is still needed to find balance. Otherwise, lawyers and professional staff will find themselves working as hard as ever – just at home instead of at the office.[363]

"Irregular working hours have become the norm for legal professionals."[364] This comes at a cost – as lawyers work more hours outside the conventional workday, their mental health and job satisfaction rates drop, which translates to burnout and attrition.[365] It is not just the billable requirements creating the excess hours. Rather, it's how the hours are allocated and what is expected to be accomplished 'off the clock'.[366] Associates often feel pressured (or are required) to take on non-billable tasks, which means their hours billed only reflect a portion of their time spent working.[367]

Being mindful of what is being asked of lawyers beyond their billable tasks could help ensure that lawyers have meaningful time to spend on life outside of the office. This balance improves overall satisfaction and reduces fatigue, both essential components of lawyer well-being.

Law firms also need to look at how they are defining and rewarding success – and success isn't only about how many hours are worked. According to Tracy LaLonde, workforce engagement expert at Joyachiever: "Putting billable hours on a pedestal is a bit like awarding a gold medal to the athlete who spent the most time training, even though they came in fifth place."[368] Embracing other drivers of performance can increase employee engagement and reduce the likelihood of burnout.[369]

At the end of the billable year, be sure that your review process offers lawyers the opportunity to present a full picture of where their time is going, and the meaningful contributions made beyond what their hours reflect – and reward these efforts.

4.12 The need to disconnect and sleep

Given the substantial pressures and often unrelenting nature of law practice, taking time off and being able to fully disconnect are critical to avoiding burnout. Yet a substantial number of lawyers don't feel comfortable taking the precious time off they are given.[370] Among the top reasons cited are the following:

- not letting work pile up;
- missing billable time;
- demanding clients; and

- for nearly half of lawyers who skipped vacation time, personal feelings of guilt.[371]

The overwhelming number of lawyers feeling guilty signals that a shift may be needed from leadership towards making clear that taking time off is expected and encouraged, rather than a sign of disloyalty and selfishness. Without meaningful breaks, the pace of law practice may be unsustainable and detrimental to the well-being of many.

In addition, the impact of sleep deprivation on performance and well-being should not be ignored. Going without sleep has an immediate impact on multiple types of thinking and brain function, reduces attention span and concentration, and diminishes mental place-keeping.[372] Studies have found that pulling an all-nighter causes impairment that is comparable to being drunk.[373] Long term, lack of sleep is associated with chronic health problems like diabetes, high blood pressure, stroke, obesity, depression and heart and kidney disease.[374]

4.13 Key takeaways

Supporting well-being initiatives and offering flexibility are crucial components of culture building that signal to your workforce that they matter. Focus on:

- developing thoughtful return-to-office practices;
- creating psychosocial safety – doing work differently;
- removing the stigma of mental health issues; and
- implementing practices that support meaningful breaks and time away.

V. Relationships, engagement and collegiality

1. What it is and why it matters

Creating and nurturing a law firm culture that supports lawyers and professional staff (both as professionals and as human beings) and treats everyone fairly is critical to a firm's success.[375] This sounds simple enough, yet something is amiss in many firms today.

> *A mix of subtle and seismic factors, including demand volatility, hybrid office work arrangements, and generational and technological shifts, have prompted the drop in motivation and fulfilment at law firms, which some analysts have called a 'huge concern'.*[376]

Addressing this disengagement is vital to reviving and maintaining a thriving workforce.

While current economic uncertainty may have brought formal closure to the Great Resignation, many of the underpinnings that drove these significant career moves remain.[377] There are a number of recent surveys that suggest workers still want to quit. LinkedIn estimated that 61% of US workers considered leaving their jobs in 2023.[378]

Trust also evaporated.[379] A 2022 survey of 5,000 US workers found that nearly one in five trusted their employers less than they did before the pandemic, and a 2023 survey found that 66% of all workers, and 83% who had recently been laid off, had lost trust in the stability and security of full-time employment.[380]

This dissatisfaction and lack of trust has created a new approach to work, according to behavioural scientist Laurel McKenzie.[381] "People are more focused," he says, "on taking care of themselves and finding organizations that will enable that."[382] They are willing to leave and find something better. The sense of loyalty to organisations is not there anymore.[383]

The need to refocus on creating and maintaining a law firm culture that fosters a sense of community, purpose and trust is essential to combating this sentiment, felt by much of the workforce. It is important to be reminded that "[e]ngagement is an outcome, not a program or list of headline-grabbing benefits".[384] It is about forming connections and creating a sense of belonging and shared goals. Yet, achieving a sense of collegiality and enthusiasm will take some creativity in the new hybrid work environment. Rather than forcing lawyers and professional staff back to in-person work to establish connections, leaders who are able to build intentional connections among employees across geographic – and generational – boundaries will reap the greatest cultural (and economic) benefits.[385]

While some in-office time may help bolster engagement, focusing solely on physical presence misses the mark. Engaging with colleagues on a human level and creating a safe work environment will have a much greater impact on employee satisfaction and a positive work culture.

And the economic benefits are real. A high sense of belonging has been linked to a 56% increase in job performance, a 50% drop in turnover risk and a 75% reduction in sick days.[386] Establishing friendships at work also promotes retention and other positive workplace characteristics, including engagement, contentment and better health.[387] "What's more, employees who report having friends at work have higher levels of productivity, retention and job satisfaction than those who don't."[388] Ultimately, these efforts are about genuine human connection and understanding and they are integral to a positive firm culture.

2. Considerations in a hybrid work environment

As firms work to reinvigorate their workforce, it is worthwhile giving consideration to how hybrid arrangements and continued virtual interactions impact relationships and engagement. Conflicting perspectives on remote and hybrid work seem to be contributing to the current tension, which in turn seems to be escalating.[389] Listening to the needs of lawyers and professional staff as individuals, finding connection points and creating a sense of common purpose will be key to overcoming the current detachment, distrust and divide.

2.1 In-office engagement

As mentioned above, the "level of energy and enthusiasm for work has dropped since the onset of the pandemic, and research shows some level of in-office work can benefit engagement".[390] Specifically, those who spend two to three days in the office have the highest levels of engagement.[391] The sweet spot seems to be a mix of both time in and away from the office – a hybrid work schedule.

However, we must not overstate the impact of in-office attendance on increased levels of engagement. "Office attendance isn't a guarantee of collaboration and cultural cohesion. A lawyer who self-isolates in their office misses the benefits of coming in."[392] Sincere relationship building and driving engagement require intentional interactions.

According to Marcie Borgal Shunk, in-office time is "notably less relevant than other factors". Autonomy, purpose, feeling valued, meaningful work, a sense of belonging, psychological safety, cohesiveness and connection contribute more to an individual's level of engagement.[393] Moreover, none of these "emanate solely from face-to-face interactions".[394] For example, team collaboration can be highly effective with a small fraction of members' time spent together in person.[395]

While some in-office time may help bolster engagement, focusing solely on physical presence misses the mark. Engaging with colleagues on a human level and creating a safe work environment will have a much greater impact on employee satisfaction and a positive work culture.

2.2 Remote and hybrid concerns

While many of us relied on various technological platforms to stay virtually connected during the pandemic, early research suggests that the benefits of these virtual activities to overcome loneliness and disconnection tend to fade fairly quickly.[396] Research also shows that lack of close contact reduces connection and trust, essential elements of healthy relationships.[397] Finding opportunities to connect in person, whether through training, client needs or social events could help alleviate some of these feelings of separation.

2.3 Harmful virtual exchanges and (undetected) virtual microaggressions

As Mark Mortensen, associate professor of organisational behaviour at the European Institute of Business Administration (INSEAD) has explained, some aspects of hybrid and remote work make harmful exchanges more likely to occur.[398] Working in a hybrid environment means a significant amount of communication will continue to take place across virtual technologies like email, text and video:

> *One of the early findings in research on the effects of technology-mediated communication is that people become more disinhibited and exhibit less self-monitoring and self-control when communicating through technology.*[399]

Put simply, when we talk to one another electronically, it is more likely that hurtful comments will come out.[400] Given that technology-mediated communication is here to stay, this is another area where proper training and awareness are essential to reducing harmful virtual exchanges.

Detecting microaggression can also be more difficult in remote and hybrid environments.[401] According to Ella Washington, founder and CEO of Ellavate Solutions, microaggression is when someone says or does something – without necessarily realising it – that feels hostile or offensive to some aspect of our identity.[402] It can be an insensitive statement, question or assumption that can target many aspects of who we are, such as our race, gender, sexuality, parental status, socioeconomic background, mental health, or any other aspect of our identity.[403]

Mortensen says that although remote and hybrid settings may have "fewer touchpoints where microaggressions can occur, they do not remove the underpinnings of why microaggressions happen – nor do they prevent them from coming out in other outlets".[404] He noted that hybrid work can obscure the problem without resolving it.[405]

While hybrid work does not necessarily cause toxicity any more than

Given that technology-mediated communication is here to stay, this is another area where proper training and awareness are essential to reducing harmful virtual exchanges.

in-person work does, Mortensen advised that it is important to recognise that hybrid environments introduce some different mechanisms through which toxicity may arise.[406] Being aware of the potential new channels for harm can help leaders recognise, protect against and eliminate toxicity when it occurs.[407]

2.4 In-office mandate cautions

> *Don't mistake presence for performance. Showing up is not a sign of commitment or contribution. It's an act of compliance.*[408]

Research strongly suggests that law firm strategies designed around encouraging connections among employees are more likely to be successful than punitive approaches.[409] Employees whose jobs can be done remotely, but who are required to come into the office, are less engaged, not more.[410] And lack of engagement is costly. "Gallup estimates low employee engagement cost $7.8 trillion in lost productivity [in 2022] – a whopping 11% of global GDP."[411] According to Shunk, leaders and firms who embrace the underlying factors driving engagement – genuine connections and a sense of belonging and purpose – rather than mandate physical presence will achieve better results.[412]

3. Generational considerations

As firms consider ways to rebuild and enhance their cultures, it is important to acknowledge the perspective of the younger generations and how they view relationship building and the importance of a work environment. "Distinct contrasts [between generations] in ways of working, personal motivators and prevailing attitudes have left many firm leaders frustrated and disillusioned when trying to integrate new hires into the law firm business model."[413] Yet a law firm leader's ability to understand and adapt to some of these generational preferences can "alleviate the palpable tension over behaviour-expectation gaps across generations," suggests Shunk.[414] Rather than succumb to the natural tendency to form opinions and make decisions based on one's own life experience, it is important to consider sound research and differing generational perspectives to find solutions that suit the unique circumstances of each generation in the office.[415]

3.1 Different communication

Differences in communication styles preferred by different generations prevent some more senior lawyers from engaging in the dialogue needed to understand, appreciate and work through those differences.[416] Newer generations do not believe in-person interactions are needed to build strong relationships, or for learning,[417] whereas

Leveraging technology will continue to play a role in creating a sense of community across geographic areas and hybrid schedules. However, the benefits of in-person interaction should not be neglected.

their Boomer and Gen X counterparts value in-person connections and developed as lawyers sitting side by side with their superiors. Both approaches have value and need not be mutually exclusive. Rather, finding a combination of both preferences may provide the recipe for optimal communication across generational differences. The key is communicating these preferences and then finding a solution that suits everyone involved.

3.2 Different normal

"Many young professionals who experienced a home office during the pandemic see hybrid work as the norm, as they have never known a different way of working," according to Nicole de Fontaines.[418] She went on to say: "In actual fact, it is a coincidence that Gen Z's expectations have been met by the unexpected generalization of hybrid work."[419] Recognising this generation's 'normal' can help inform how law firm leaders approach any adjustments to their hybrid work policies and how they might be received. Remote work was a significant adjustment for the existing workforce, and now in-person attendance is asking Gen Z to make a similar shift in how they are accustomed to working.

3.3 Different preferences, sort of

Differing generational experiences have also led to divergent approaches to colleagues and careers. Shunk provides a helpful overview of generational preferences and where commonality might be found.[420] She explains that Boomers value loyalty to the team and are motivated by collective action and decisions with those around them. This loyalty aligns with that of Millennials, who are loyal to peers and place value in fairness, inclusivity and equal treatment. However, these generations perceive authority differently – Boomers respect authority inherently, while authority for Millennials must be earned. The generation sandwiched in between, Gen X, operates largely independently, and most often shows loyalty to superiors and values results, at times to the detriment of relationships. Lastly, Gen Zers are purpose-driven and their loyalty is to the experience and how it contributes to their growth. Engagement for each generation requires approaches that most align with their values.[421]

4. Change management

Ultimately, a firm's culture is created by the forming of meaningful relationships among colleagues and clients. And it is firm leaders who must help establish norms of working that foster engagement and inclusion for the entire workforce. Leveraging technology will continue to play a role in creating a sense of community across geographic areas and hybrid schedules. However, the benefits of in-person interaction should not be neglected.

4.1 Keep connecting

Developing personal connections with colleagues and managers is foundational to a strong sense of culture. "The more connected teams are, the more they trust, collaborate and elevate the performance of one another."[422] Firms that invest the time for managers and teams to connect and get to know one another on a personal level, regardless of where they work, will reap the cultural benefits.

With more limited opportunity for such interactions to occur spontaneously, firms committed to creating intentional spaces for casual connection and relationship building will reap the rewards of greater cohesiveness.

Tips for continued connection building

Some successful practices firms undertook at the start of the pandemic that are still valuable in the hybrid era include:

- scheduling time at the beginning of team meetings for informal chatting and ice-breakers;
- establishing open-invitation office hours in which leaders are available online (and in person) and welcome people dropping in;
- asking people for ideas about how they like to connect; and
- creating spaces, using online collaboration tools, that are dedicated to fun topics and casual chatting.

4.2 Create more channels

Firms that offer a variety of channels for lawyers and professional staff to provide ongoing feedback and ways to get support show they are listening and committed to the well-being of their workforce. Some ways to do this include:

- periodic surveys regarding wellness and satisfaction;
- feedback questionnaires to evaluate the effectiveness of programmes and resources;
- dedicated channels for employees to ask for resources they need and an emphasis on the safety of asking; and
- ongoing ways for confidential upward feedback, when it would be beneficial for matters to be addressed more urgently.

4.3 Empathy and psychological safety

One of the most effective tools you can put in place is a culture with "built-in antibodies against toxic behaviors", says Mortensen.[423] "In particular, focus on promoting empathy and psychological safety."[424] A culture with empathy at its core encourages employees to consider the impact of their actions on their co-workers, which increases the likelihood that employees will catch themselves before behaving in a way another might find upsetting. Psychological safety is "critical" for those instances that "empathy doesn't prevent".[425]

4.4 High-value interactions

Kristin Stark, law firm consultant and principal at Fairfax Associates Law, suggests that firms can cultivate better engagement at all levels by focusing on what she calls "high-value interactions" and reducing "low-value ones".[426] Put into practice, this means eliminating those meetings (virtual or in-person) that leave people saying to themselves, "This could have been an email".[427] To successfully create high-value exchanges among colleagues, Gartner research suggests that employers focus on three elements:

- employee choice and autonomy;
- a clear structure and purpose; and
- a sense of levity and fun.[428]

Make interactions meaningful and engaging, not just a transfer of information.

4.5 Structure unstructured time

Shunk advises that, given the new reality of how we work and the geographic bounds of many law firms, finding ways to interact in a casual manner may require that we intentionally build in conducive moments – essentially, structure unstructured time.[429] Pick up the phone and ask how someone is doing, encourage personal shares and informal conversation at the beginning of meetings, and make the effort to spend time together outside the office – everyone needs to eat lunch.[430]

4.6 It's okay to disagree

As we all adjust to this new sense of normal, there may be a tendency to tiptoe around each other as we test out ways to best interact. However, Shunk reminds us that the "absence of disagreement is not a sign of engagement or positive culture – quite the opposite".[431] Lack of dissent may suggest that a firm culture does not tolerate differing perspectives, questioning of leadership or the space for failure. Conflict, when it arises in a respectful manner, is a sign of a normal and healthy work culture. Focus should be placed on training partners and managers to lead constructive dialogue and normalise and support disagreement to advance the team, and drive engagement.[432]

4.7 Keep it casual

Large law firms have long tended to have fairly formal cultures. Remote work created a more relaxed environment, which allowed for personal connection. We have now seen dogs and children in the background of Zoom meetings, and have had windows into the personal lives of our colleagues never experienced before. The humanisation of our peers has been an unexpected exercise in shifting away from formal law culture, and its momentum should be continued as we move forward.

4.8 Include everyone

Last, but certainly not least, are the benefits of bringing all personnel together. Breaking down the barriers between lawyers and professional staff and allowing for meaningful connections to occur between everyone at the firm will foster a cohesive and strong sense of culture and promote engagement at all levels.

4.9 Key takeaways

How we engage and the relationships we form at work matter. They are central elements of culture building. Focus on:

- creating opportunities for meaningful connection;
- eliminating toxicity and microagressions;
- removing antiquated formalities; and
- including everyone in the office – lawyers and professional staff.

VI. Diversity, inclusion and belonging

1. What it is and why it matters

Let's quickly define what diversity, inclusion and belonging (DIB) means in the context of this special report:

- 'Diversity' captures who is represented in the workforce.[433]
- 'Inclusion' refers to how the workforce experiences the workplace and the extent to which organisations embrace all employees and enable them to make meaningful contributions.[434]
- 'Belonging' is a feeling of community with the people and environments that make us feel connected.[435]

Advancing DIB has long been central to sustaining a healthy law firm culture, and efforts made by firms over the years have made an impact. However, deep disparities remain, especially at the leadership level. According to the 2023 American Bar Association (ABA) *Profile of the Legal Profession*, racial and ethnic under-representation in the legal profession continues to be alarming.[436] Just over 13% of the US population is Black. Only 4.5% of US lawyers are Black. And while 19% of the US population is Hispanic, just 6% of all US lawyers are Hispanic. And 1.3% of the US population is Native American or Alaska Native, but only 0.5% of US lawyers are Native American or Alaska Native.[437]

Moreover, in the United States, 70% of Black women lawyers have experienced or witnessed discrimination or bias in their workplace and 47% feel burdened to educate others about DIB issues, according to a recent survey by Kanarys Inc and the Women Lawyers Division.[438] Nearly 20% of Black women lawyers also reported that they do not feel like they belong at their organisation.[439]

There are some signs of progress. In recent years, the legal profession has attracted more students from diverse backgrounds. In the United States, the incoming class of 2022 was the most diverse ever, with 39% of students identifying as persons of colour, an increase from the 36.9% in 2021 (which was a record at the time).[440] Data indicating that the 2023 incoming class would be even more racially and ethnically diverse turned out to be accurate.[441]

While this momentum is encouraging, the recent US Supreme Court's decisions in *SFFA v Harvard* and *SFFA v UNC* effectively eliminated the use of affirmative action in college admissions. "[C]ase studies suggest that when universities eliminate affirmative action, they produce a less diverse candidate pool for employers to tap."[442] US law firms need to consider the effect that this, and any future judicial rulings and state legislation, will have on their recruiting efforts.[443] However, they should

Firms should stay the course in building diverse firms that offer a variety of perspectives and reflect a country's population and its juries.

not expand the reach of the decision further than necessary. Firms should stay the course in building diverse firms that offer a variety of perspectives and reflect a country's population and its juries.

It appears that most US corporate DIB programmes are formally safe for now, but organisations should be mindful of the changing landscape.[444] Recent lawsuits filed by conservative legal activist Edward Blum alleging reverse racism against Perkins Coie, Morrison Foerster, and Winston and Strawn – with potentially more to follow – have prompted some Big Law firms to carefully scrutinise their DIB measures.[445] According to Joelle Emerson, co-founder and CEO of Paradigm: "There seems to be a pause on many of the efforts firms were engaged in – even efforts that pose no risk."[446] Firms are also performing some risk management on programmes that were already lawful by adding race-neutral language and eliminating criteria that specify under-represented groups.[447]

The importance of continuing these efforts can't be emphasised enough. In addition to the moral reasons for supporting DIB programmes, the business case also remains compelling. Diverse teams benefit organisational performance. "Ample research shows that they make smarter decisions and better investments, are more adaptable, and drive innovation."[448] Moreover, "inclusive organizations are 73% more likely to reap innovation revenue, 70% more likely to capture new markets, up to 50% more likely to make better decisions, and up to 36% more likely to have above-average profitability".[449] However, in order to do so, the corporate culture in which they operate needs to be a supportive, psychologically safe one.[450] Diverse and well-trained employees and leadership teams are also better equipped to interact with diverse employees and clients.[451]

2. Considerations in a hybrid work environment

Hybrid work has provided some shelter and sought-after flexibility for under-represented groups, and caregivers in particular. As firms navigate whether to continue with this flexibility, they should be aware of the heightened impacts on these particular individuals.

2.1 In-office consequences for under-represented groups

When refining in-office and flexible work programmes, it is important to consider that marginalised groups, especially communities of colour, have shown a particular interest in not returning to a workplace where they frequently experienced bias from co-workers.[452] While firms work to eliminate bias and improve their work environments, it is important that under-represented groups continue to have work arrangements that make them feel heard and supported.

Hybrid and remote work arrangements are also highly valued by women, who still typically serve as the primary caregivers in households.[453] The shift by some firms to require a return to the office could be perceived as being hostile to women and families.[454] Caregivers are faced with a difficult choice between flexibility and potential career advancement.[455] These policies could result in attrition, thereby limiting the talent pool and the overall diversity of the firm.[456]

2.2 Equalising work access

Some argue that hybrid policies could "force law firms to be more organized with the assignment of work, which should result in a more equitable allocation among junior lawyers".[457] However, there is another concern – that hybrid work will afford those who are able to be in the office greater access to assignments by their sheer physical presence. Given the remote work preference of marginalised communities and caregivers, this in-person work allocation could have a disproportionately negative impact on these groups.

3. Generational considerations

As we've said before, members of each generation see things from different perspectives. This is as true for DIB as it is for anything else.[458] To create workplace harmony that leads to effective collaboration and high performance, it is important for each generation to understand how others perceive what diversity means.[459]

3.1 Different definitions of diversity and inclusion

Millennials and Gen Zers view diversity at work differently than their older colleagues. Gen Z has the most expansive views yet, including their take on identity and orientation.[460] Diversity is a broader concept to these generations than just physical traits.[461] They are "more likely to define diversity as a mix of experiences, identities, ideas and opinions, rather than a more traditional definition of diversity".[462] Millennials and Gen Zers' notion of diversity is really cognitive diversity, which is about considering experiences, identities and opinions in the workplace as a source of innovation.[463] Inclusion is about having a culture of connectedness that encourages teambuilding, collaboration and professional growth.[464]

This differs from prior generations who traditionally consider diversity from the perspectives of representation and assimilation.[465] To many Boomers, diversity is about integrating people of under-represented racial, ethnic and gender demographics into the workplace.[466] They do not necessarily consider a direct connection to business results.[467] Rather, Boomers are more likely to consider diversity a reputational issue for their firms.[468]

There has been a shift in the last decade from highly educated Millennials and Gen Zers who have increasingly prioritised personal values in deciding where to work. These cohorts expect employers to be equally committed to changing their organisations.

Many Gen Xers view diversity as a representation of – and fairness to – all individuals, no matter their demographic identifiers.[469] For Gen X, inclusion is the process by which all individuals – including those who are demographically diverse – are protected, treated fairly and afforded consistent opportunities.[470]

3.2 To Millennials and Gen Zers, diversity is a must

There has been a shift in the last decade from highly educated Millennials and Gen Zers who have increasingly prioritised personal values in deciding where to work.[471] These cohorts expect employers to be equally committed to changing their organisations. They expect a more diverse workforce, advancement support for under-represented employees, and a commitment to confronting systemic racism in their ranks. And the commitment must be genuine and authentic: "Young job seekers say they're attuned to anything that smacks of performance."[472]

4. Change management

Recent court rulings and a shifting political climate have placed DIB programmes under greater scrutiny, but leaders should also "take care to ensure their efforts to protect against legal risk don't turn into a fear-driven abandonment of effective [DIB] practices", according to diversity, equity and inclusion consultant Lily Zheng.[473] Taking into account the various challenges faced by historically marginalised communities and creating programmes that work to overcome the inherent inequities these groups face is foundational for firms advancing DIB.

Advancing DIB improves culture, and culture promotes retention and engagement. It is important to take time to evaluate where your firm stands with regard to its DIB efforts. Table 5 offers a rubric for assessing the maturity phase of an organisation's DIB strategy – and all law firms should aspire to move upward along this continuum. Below, we offer a few ideas for how to advance.

Table 5: The impact of a D&I programme[474]

Business impact	D&I maturity	
Strategic	Differentiated	Employees view D&I as essential to driving people and business performance; inclusion is naturally incorporated into all aspects of employee and customer experience.
	Progressing	Programmes, practices and infrastructure are more highly integrated with the talent life cycle. Some employees view D&I as a core competency.
	Basic	Basic programme, process and infrastructure have some alignment with the talent life cycle. A broader set of employees understand basic D&I concepts as well as their business value.
Tactical	Emerging	Rudimentary programmes exist, but are seen as separate from elements of the talent life cycle and are not linked to business needs. Some employees understand the concept of D&I.

4.1 Look at the data

Law firms need to ensure that DIB efforts are integrated into their broader strategic plans rather than relegated to a particular department's goals. And as DIB efforts become more scrutinised, it is even more important to ensure that a firm's processes are equitable.[475] Lauren Stiller Rikleen, founder and president of the Rikleen Institute for Strategic Leadership, advises that firms should pay close attention to the year-to-year statistics that show how they are performing.[476]

Performance evaluations, compensation and advancement decisions should be based on standard and objective data.[477] However, research indicates that they remain riddled with systemic bias.[478] Oxford Reference defines systemic or institutional bias as a "tendency for the procedures and practices of particular institutions to operate in ways which result in certain social groups being advantaged or favored and others being disadvantaged or devalued".[479] To combat this bias, firms need to focus on changing their systems, not individuals.[480] One reason unconscious bias training programmes fail to be effective in creating lasting change is that they focus on changing individual behaviours while leaving largely untouched the systems that enabled those behaviours to thrive.[481] When people look at a problem from a systems-level perspective they are more motivated to actually want to fix the problem – the system provides more room to intervene rather than just punish individuals.[482] It is worthwhile for firms to audit their processes and confirm that they are not favouring one group over another.[483] When DIB becomes incorporated into the lifeblood of the organisation, the relevant data will support this.[484]

4.2 Support clients

Clients are also re-examining their current DIB initiatives and will be looking to their law firms for support. "There's a real need for practical, creative guidance right now," says Jason Schwartz, partner and labour and employment co-chair at Gibson, Dunn & Crutcher.[485] Gibson addressed this need with the formation of a diversity, equity and inclusion task force to service increased client demand for diversity and inclusion compliance.[486] Whether through task forces, client alerts or proactive outreach, helping clients navigate DIB in the current climate ensures the sustainability of these vital corporate programmes.

4.3 Where are you recruiting?

With the US Supreme Court's recent dismantling of affirmative action in universities, firms should re-examine the breadth of the schools they recruit from. In-house counsels say they will be watching this as well.[487] Knowing which schools firm leaders recruit from gives insight into how seriously a firm thinks about attracting a diverse pool of candidates, according to Rhonda Powell, general counsel at non-profit Strada Education Network.[488]

Recruiting new lawyers – especially in light of recent US Supreme Court decisions – only from select law schools is seen as a key contributing factor in reducing diversity at large law firms. In an effort to combat some of the flaws in hiring practices, some law firms have begun to leverage AI with a view to broadening their range of schools and applicant pool.

4.4 Artificial intelligence (AI)

The recruiting process for new associates has a significant impact on the diversity of a firm's workforce. Recruiting new lawyers – especially in light of recent US Supreme Court decisions – only from select law schools is seen as a key contributing factor in reducing diversity at large law firms. In an effort to combat some of the flaws in hiring practices, some law firms have begun to leverage AI with a view to broadening their range of schools and applicant pool.

As with any new tool, it is important to proceed with caution. At first glance, AI and job hiring appear to be "a match made in employment equity heaven".[489] There is hope that these algorithms can focus on skills and exclude identifiers that might trigger unconscious bias, such as name, gender, age and education.[490] Some AI recruiting products have already proved there are ways to do this. It is important to identify where the risks are to ensure that AI tools are being selected and used in a way that is non-discriminatory and can expand the talent pool.[491]

Governments are also starting to take notice of the potential concerns of AI use in hiring. As of 5 July 2023, a law in New York City went into effect which "requires employers that use AI and other machine learning technology as part of their hiring process to perform an annual audit of their recruitment technology".[492] The audits are required to be performed by a third party and check for instances of bias built into these systems.[493]

4.5 Structure is good

Creating more structure around mentoring programmes ensures more equal access to opportunities.[494] Avoid "'match like with like' to provide more opportunities for all younger lawyers to work with the most powerful and influential group in law, which consists mostly of white male partners".[495] If you only pair women of colour with women of colour, you are missing opportunities for relationship building between those senior men and women of colour, according to Rachael Bosch, founder and managing director of Fringe Professional Development. You are also adding an extra layer of burden to the very few senior leaders who are women of colour.[496]

Formalising workflows also ensures that hours are evenly apportioned and all lawyers have equalised access to interesting and challenging work. This enables lawyers of all races, genders and identities to grow as professionals and advance their careers.

4.6 Consider everyone

When structuring diversity and inclusion programmes, it is important to consider everyone at the firm – professional staff as well as lawyers.

Historically, these programmes have not included professional staff, which is a missed opportunity and fails to include a large segment of the workforce.[497] Making space for true representation and belonging can only be achieved when everyone is included.

4.7 Create belonging

Creating a sense of belonging is a critical component of advancing diversity and inclusion initiatives. And psychological safety is what makes an employee feel like they belong.[498] When someone feels psychologically safe, they believe others will give them the benefit of the doubt and they can ask questions and raise issues without fear.[499] This sense of safety and belonging is what creates the most high-performing teams, where members can innovate and learn and grow together.[500]

4.8 Listen

There is so much to learn by simply listening. "Listening is an action," says Michael Coston, CEO of business advisory firm Coston Consulting.[501] "When it comes to the [DIB] space, it's one of the most important things you can do."[502] Leaders who take the time to actually listen to what their diverse lawyers and professional staff think of their organisation and what individuals have experienced while working there enable firms to incorporate concerns into action plans that can make a meaningful difference. Smarter firms design their offerings in "active collaboration" with their workforce.[503]

4.9 Universal diversity and inclusion

A newer way to reframe a firm's approach to DIB is to use a universal approach, instead of interventions targeted at specific demographic groups.[504] Universal approaches may be useful in places resistant to continuing more specialised programming. They are 'legally safe' strategies because they stand to benefit everyone, including members of historically dominant groups. They focus on creating space for greater authenticity and self-expression, and for increased psychological safety. While everyone benefits from these efforts, marginalised individuals will reap the greatest benefits, as they are the ones who feel most excluded from workplaces without such initiatives.[505]

In order to create the conditions for all workers to thrive, Laura Morgan Roberts, associate professor of business administration at the University of Virginia's Darden School of Business, advises that workplaces need to cultivate four freedoms that allow people to "bring their full humanity to work".[506] These include:

- being our authentic selves;
- becoming our best selves;

- occasionally fading into the background; and
- failing in ways that help us and our teams learn.[507]

Being oneself at work may sound simple, but creating the freedom to do so takes continued efforts to establish and uphold non-discrimination policies, anti-bias programming and allyship.[508]

Becoming our best selves also involves the practice of improving oneself and one's situation. Research has shown that those in marginalised groups are exposed to a 'praise deficit' and managers often subject workers from historically under-represented groups to more scrutiny and give them less recognition for demonstrated success.[509] To combat this, companies need to establish high-quality development programmes that are accessible to all and need to train managers to give more constructive and objective feedback to everyone.[510]

The third freedom is about being able to step back and take a break from the performance pressure.[511] Many in marginalised groups experience hypervisibility, which results in being judged more harshly for perceived failures or deviations from the norm. Increasing diversity allows those in marginalised groups the ability to fade into the background or to blend in to escape scrutiny.[512]

Being oneself at work may sound simple, but creating the freedom to do so takes continued efforts to establish and uphold non-discrimination policies, anti-bias programming and allyship.

The last freedom is to fail – and it is the most important because pursuing the other freedoms involves some risk.[513] Knowing there is the opportunity to recover helps everyone embrace the four freedoms with greater confidence.[514]

4.10 Key takeaways

Diversity, inclusion and belonging remain central components of a thriving law firm culture. And more work needs to be done. Focus on:

- being mindful of the changing landscape;
- addressing systemic bias;
- adjusting recruiting practices;
- using AI cautiously;
- listening, and creating belonging; and
- cultivating the four freedoms.

Essentially, it is all about "making the work work for everyone".[515]

VII. Recruiting and onboarding

1. What it is and why it matters

Recruiting top talent can be a daunting endeavour for law firms. However, it is one thing they can't skimp on "as great talent is the foundation of organizational success".[516] As we know, law firms are a people business, and its people are what sets a law firm apart.[517] Effort spent on finding a candidate who aligns with your firm culture and can propel your business forward is time well spent.

Successful recruiting and onboarding requires a thoughtful, strategic approach to sharing with candidates why it's the best next move in their career. With compensation no longer being the sole consideration for many candidates, it is critical that firms rethink their value proposition as employers, and firm culture can be the key differentiator.[518] The way a firm conducts interviewing, hiring and onboarding establishes its culture in the eyes of a potential hire. And, as with many other areas of law firms, the recruitment journey may look a little different than it did pre-pandemic.

Legal hiring and demand hit record levels over the past few years as the economy rebounded and the industry faced pent-up demand from the initial impacts of the pandemic.[519] With the market now cooling, law firms are wisely "recalibrating their strategic plans based on what they think is best for their business rather than on perceived talent supply famine in the marketplace".[520] However, strong demand remains for skilled lawyers who are the right fit for organisations.

2. Considerations in a hybrid work environment

Hybrid considerations with regard to recruiting and onboarding have both cultural and practical components which should be explored, as both may assist in effectively recruiting top talent. Firms also need to be aware that the seamlessness of working remotely has increased the mobility of lawyers – and entire practice groups.

2.1 Most are looking for flexibility

In our new era of hybrid work, flexibility and in-office attendance policies have become one of the central components defining a firm's culture. It is top of mind (sometimes even above compensation) for most candidates. How a law firm defines and presents its office attendance approach may be a defining moment in a candidate's selection of firm.

Even as the talent market cools, sought-after candidates will still have the ability to pick and choose the firm environment that best suits their lifestyle and professional goals. Flexibility still seems to be key when recruiting most talent. "[T]here has been a real shift in terms of

How a law firm defines and presents its office attendance approach may be a defining moment in a candidate's selection of firm.

how lawyers want to work in the future," says Roberta Liebenberg, a principal with Chicago-based Red Bee Group.[521] In an ABA report from 2022, young lawyers felt "so strongly about remote work that 44% of them would leave their current jobs for a greater ability to work remotely elsewhere".[522] Flexible and remote work are also preferred by most women, with 56% reporting that remote work increased their ability to balance work and family obligations.[523]

While attendance policies appear to be following some geographic patterns in the United States, remote options and increased mobility no longer limit candidates to their place of residence. For firms seeking to recruit top talent, "the preference to work remotely among a large segment of young lawyers is a new reality of work".[524] Firms that want to attract the best should be prepared to address the issue and, when not offering hybrid or remote work options, have a meaningful alternative and a compelling reason for not doing so.[525]

2.2 Lateral (and new lawyer) recruitment and onboarding made easier

There are practical advantages to our new hybrid moment when it comes to recruiting. The prevalence and acceptance of video conferencing enables firms and candidates to meet virtually, at least at the outset, to determine whether employment should be pursued. The cost and time savings of utilising these virtual methods is significant. Several firms are utilising initial virtual interviews for lateral and new associate hiring as well.

The American Lawyer noted that lateral hiring at the partner level generally took at least six months due to the time required for lawyers to visit offices in person for multiple meetings and meet-and-greet sessions, but the ability to conduct remote meetings shortened that process to as little as six weeks.[526] Previously, lateral hires would come out of the recruiting process exhausted.[527] "You've been on airplanes for months, you're meeting tons of people. Now, candidates go into the onboarding process a lot more fresh than they did in the old days," says San Francisco-based legal recruiter Avis Caravello.[528] Reducing the timeline for lateral hiring and simplifying the process thanks to virtual technology is a welcome change in recruiting.

Intentionality will also be key in helping laterals transition and feel integrated at their new firm and continue their ongoing learning and growth. The effort should begin from the start of their tenure. Clear and well-developed shared expectations, goal setting, lateral-specific mentoring, the strategic use of technology to foster and quickly develop relationships across offices, and swift lateral inclusion in business development initiatives are all good tools for successful lateral onboarding.

Clear and well-developed shared expectations, goal setting, lateral-specific mentoring, the strategic use of technology to foster and quickly develop relationships across offices, and swift lateral inclusion in business development initiatives are all good tools for successful lateral onboarding.

2.3 Group mobility

Hybrid and remote work have enabled new alliances to form across offices, sometimes at the expense of the ties that used to bind lawyers with regular office attendance.[529] Relationships between attorneys based in different locations have grown tighter in the last few years, according to Pittsburgh-based legal recruiter Maura McAnney.[530] Remote work has also allowed groups to develop that might not have otherwise.[531] And these geographically diverse groups have become mobile. Law firm leaders have become more comfortable with hiring practice groups based in multiple jurisdictions.[532] They allow a firm to expedite growth in a practice "with a ready-made team of practitioners and clients".[533]

Onboarding is also expedited, says Teresa Bult, administrative partner and general counsel for Constangy Brooks, as there is no longer a need to open an office everywhere a firm has lawyers and professional staff.[534] The "major" logistical hurdle firms now face is making sure everyone has a computer in their hands when they arrive at the firm.[535]

In a hiring environment where entire practices are being lifted out of a firm, the importance of fostering a "cohesive and well-integrated firm that's on the same page about aspirations for the future" is all the more important, according to Kent Zimmermann, partner and law firm consultant at the Zeughauser Group.[536] The risk of one lawyer feeling like a firm isn't the right fit and moving on has now expanded to entire practice groups being able to make the move together.

3. Generational considerations

As discussed, there are prevailing mindsets in each generation, shaped by their early careers and the workplace culture that came before them.[537] These differences impact what each generation values and looks for from their work environment. The most concerning generational consideration as it applies to recruiting is convincing the youngest generation of lawyers to join Big Law in the first place. The desire to join a Big Law firm after law school graduation has decreased among future Gen Z lawyers.[538] In a 2023 survey from Major, Lindsey & Africa, while 70% of respondents said they plan to pursue the law firm track, only 39% said they would join a Big Law firm, down significantly from 59% who said the same in the 2020 version of the survey.[539] And it doesn't appear that this generation has plans to stay in Big Law. A combined 53% of Gen Z respondents said they were interested in eventually transitioning to an in-house, government, or non-profit position, in comparison to 23% who aspire to make partner at a law firm.[540]

3.1 What Gen Z wants

Gen Zers give more weight to non-monetary factors than most of their predecessors. The Major, Lindsey & Africa survey found that formal mentorship and training tied compensation as the most important factors for Gen Z in selecting a law firm.[541] Gen Z also noted that an open-door environment and informal day-to-day training are also important.[542]

Gen Zers are also concerned with the moral values and political leanings of their prospective employers. "Associates in particular – but also partners – want their firms to stand for something."[543] This generation wants to work for businesses that mirror their own values around equality, diversity and sustainability.[544] Sixty per cent of respondents to the Major, Lindsey & Africa survey noted that corporate responsibility programmes were important in their selection of a potential employer, and 63% reported that an organisation's social justice priorities would impact their decision-making process.[545] In the past, law firms went out of their way to be politically neutral. Now, they're more likely to take public stances and speak out – a welcome change for the younger generations.[546] To attract young talent, ensure you make it easy for Gen Z candidates to access information on your company values and how you enact those values.[547]

3.2 Who wants to be a partner?

Kristin Stark aptly noted:

> *Law firm leaders are grappling with the fact that kind of the grand bargain has changed between law firms and associates and partners and associates because most associates are not aiming to build a career at these law firms.*[548]

The prospect of becoming an equity partner is no longer motivating many junior lawyers.[549] Millennials and Gen Z lawyers are placing greater emphasis on mental health and flexibility, and less emphasis, in the words of Daniel Farris, partner-in-charge of the Chicago office of Norton Rose Fulbright, on "the pie-eating contest where the reward is more pie".[550]

As discussed earlier, there is some recent evidence to suggest that Millennials may be more inclined to seek partnership; nevertheless, turnover rates at law firms have been alarming over the past few years.[551] A *Thomson Reuters* legal industry report measured the associate turnover rate at nearly 25% at the end of 2021, and it remained at 20.1% in 2022 which, according to Stark, is "one of the higher levels that we have seen in the past decade".[552] Recent studies suggest that turnover rates may be returning to 2019 levels in the broader workforce, though how this plays out at law firms remains to be seen.[553]

At the end of the day, there needs to be a shift in how Gen Z (and some Millennials) view a career in Big Law.[554] Rather than seeing it as a burden, younger lawyers need to feel like a Big Law career is a privilege, which allows them to do "high-quality work for high-quality clients, alongside high-quality colleagues".[555] Otherwise, the constant churn will continue to erode the long-term viability and success of Big Law firms.

4. Change management

As law firms reevaluate how to retain and attract top talent, it is essential that they have a solid grasp of who they are and identify the strengths and weaknesses of their employer brand.[556] A recent ABA report identified the factors that lawyers consider most important when deciding to change jobs.[557] "Sixty-eight per cent of female lawyers and 44% of male lawyers believe better work/life balance is important."[558] Relatedly, 68% of lawyers of colour find this balance important.[559] Also ranking high on the list for most lawyers is a more welcoming and collaborative culture, increased compensation, the ability to work remotely and better quality of work.[560] These results suggest that a firm that offers flexibility and a vibrant culture will have greater success in attracting a diverse and dynamic workforce.

4.1 Be specific about who you are as a firm

Firms can often articulate why they need a specific lawyer, but tend to struggle with why anyone should join them, according to Steve Nelson, an executive principal at The McCormick Group.[561] Referring to a strong law firm culture or using the buzzwords 'collaborative', 'collegial' or 'entrepreneurial' is not enough.[562] Firms should be very specific about what sets them apart and what they stand for.[563] Duane Cormell, co-founder and director of Realm Recruit, comments:

> *Those firms that have a thorough sense of what they're about and take steps towards strengthening and properly communicating their culture will be in a strong position to compete for talent.*[564]

Taking important leadership time to define (or redefine) what a firm represents as an organisation is a critical first step in shaping firm culture and communicating this in recruiting programmes.

4.2 Articulate your purpose

Younger lawyers also value a sense of meaning and purpose in their work and are committed to making a difference in the world.[565] Consider and articulate where your firm makes the biggest impact in the wider context and incorporate that into the recruitment and onboarding process.[566] Regularly showcasing work that aligns with a firm's purpose also reminds current lawyers and professional staff that what they do matters.[567]

4.3 What matters most?

The question remains: what will motivate younger lawyers to join your firm? According to Jessie Yount, companies embracing a hybrid or flexible work policy have added head count to their teams at almost twice the pace of fully in-person companies.[568] But will flexibility win out over additional compensation? Compensation remains as the most important variable for younger lawyers who are evaluating job offers.[569] However, most of them say they would be willing to sacrifice some pay for options such as additional free time, reduced billable hours, or a more flexible work schedule, according to a recent report from Major Lindsey & Africa and Above The Law.[570] While compensation still reigns as the primary driver, flexibility considerations play a significant role in the decision process as well. This represents an opportunity for firms to think creatively about how to address this dichotomy and find solutions that do not make choosing compensation or flexibility mutually exclusive.

4.4 Pay and performance transparency

And again, how compensation and promotions programmes are communicated matters. Firms that are transparent about compensation, promotion pathways and performance expectations will outperform less candid firms.[571]

While compensation still reigns as the primary driver, flexibility considerations play a significant role in the decision process as well. This represents an opportunity for firms to think creatively about how to address this dichotomy and find solutions that do not make choosing compensation or flexibility mutually exclusive.

4.5 Be specific about your policies and consider being flexible

Setting expectations and being clear about firm policies are important components to successful recruiting and onboarding efforts. In particular, be very specific about your firm's remote versus in-the-office policy.[572] Steve Nelson advises that "[i]t is no secret that most employees want flexibility and most firms are emphasizing that in their policies, but the devil is often in the details"; and that attention should also be paid to how policies are communicated, as "the articulation of your policy is as important as the policy itself".[573]

4.6 Provide resources

At the onset of the pandemic, many firms augmented their resources and training programmes in an attempt to support their lawyers and professional staff with training specific to the challenges of 2020. Lawyers continue to say that it is important for employers to provide specific resources and programmes, succession plans for leadership roles – including regular check-ins from managers – and wellness and mental health resources.[574] Notably, female lawyers, lawyers of colour and lawyers with a disability are more likely to consider these resources and offerings important than male lawyers, white lawyers and lawyers without a disability.[575]

4.7 Provide a plan

Building formalised professional development programmes is another selling point for firms to offer potential candidates. Younger lawyers are particularly interested in what career paths are available to them at the firm.

4.8 Pay for attendance?

While priorities have shifted for younger lawyers, compensation remains relevant, and it may be a factor firms can leverage when responding to inquiries about flexible work arrangements. For example, some firms that offer a hybrid schedule are offering bonuses to lawyers who elect to be in the office full-time.[576] This information is shared with caution though, as women and under-represented groups disproportionately seek out and value remote work arrangements compared to their white male counterparts,[577] which could lead to greater pay inequities along similar lines. With the trade-offs people are willing to make for flexibility, this approach may drive people into the lateral market.

4.9 Alternative billing tracks

Another way some firms are attracting those seeking more flexibility is to offer alternative billing tracks.[578] The typical hours minimum in bigger law firms is between 2,000 and 2,100 billable hours annually, with the actual hours worked by those seeking career advancement reaching 2,400 billable hours or more.[579] To appeal to the talented lawyers seeking a less rigorous schedule, firms that are offering flexibility in this area will be very attractive to lawyers seeking more control over their schedules.[580]

4.10 Keep recruiting your own lawyers

While there has been some slowdown in lateral movement, Major, Lindsey & Africa associate recruiter Kate Reder Sheikh has commented that "[B]ig Law firms shouldn't be lulled into a false sense of security".[581] Major, Lindsey & Africa recently surveyed around 300 Big Law associates and one in four respondents said they planned to leave their firms within the year, while three out of five associates felt their firms weren't actively trying to retain them. The survey found that "90% of associates would be more likely to stay if they felt their firms had made a conscious effort to retain them".[582] One method some firms are employing to try to retain talent is 'stay interviews', which help talent managers understand the evolving needs of their post-pandemic workforce.[583] Associates also selected money, firm culture and interesting work as their top three priorities, with prestige of a firm and availability of informal mentorship as their next choices.[584]

4.11 Key takeaways

Finding the right talent that advances a firm's culture and business is not an easy task. Using thoughtful recruiting and onboarding practices ensures a firm attracts great people. Focus on:

- offering flexibility;
- knowing who you are as a firm;
- using technology to conserve time and energy;
- recognising new talent wants more than just money; and
- re-recruiting your current talent.

VIII. Conclusion: embracing change

The American Lawyer recently released its A-List ranking of the "most well-rounded members" of the Am Law 200, and a common key to their success is embracing change.[585] The pandemic upended deeply held workplace norms and practices at law firms. Firms that are willing to integrate new practices and beliefs into their ecosystem of firm culture and encourage – rather than resist – this opportunity to redefine how law firms operate will create a thriving workforce and firm culture.

1. Versatile, inclusive, evolved leadership and communication
Leaders who adapt to – and embrace – shifting workplace norms and preferences will reinforce and cultivate their firm cultures. It is proactive, versatile and inclusive leadership that will help guide firms forward. Leaders must model a growth mindset and support new policies and methods to establish a more integrated and cohesive environment.

Best practices for integration and cohesion

- See change as something to be defined and led.
- Respond with a variety of styles and behaviours.
- Cultivate an inclusive environment.
- The ability to listen well and often is critical, especially as face-to-face interactions may not always be readily available. Demonstrating a genuine understanding of others will enable

leaders to build meaningful relationships with those around them.

- Demonstrate empathy and support for others. It has been an exceptionally challenging few years, and we are all still recovering from the experience. Taking the time to acknowledge individual needs, goals and challenges is instrumental in building a culture of trust and understanding.
- Provide clear, transparent and honest communication to the entire workforce. This builds trust and loyalty across the firm.
- Be mindful of proximity bias and the importance of making everyone on the team feel included, regardless of their geographic location.
- Acknowledge and adjust to generational differences that impact how individuals might interact and receive information. The younger generations value open dialogue and appreciate feedback at a regular cadence.
- Take the time to bring up new leaders at the firm. Many lawyers are ready for this next step, and creating the space for new voices will support their career advancement and ensure the long-term viability of the organisation.

Leaders who are receptive to creative new approaches to guide their workforce will make great strides towards positive culture development.

2. Refocus on talent development

The importance of building and maintaining a robust professional development programme isn't a new concept. However, the combination of burnout, career insecurity and years' worth of potentially undertrained associates makes refocusing on talent development all the more necessary today. It is vital to driving engagement and productivity, and demonstrates a commitment to the professional advancement of lawyers and professional staff at a firm.

Pay particular attention to your current (and future) Millennial leaders. The future of your firms rests on their shoulders. Listen to their needs and preferences and invest in meaningful succession planning.

There is much discussion surrounding the ability to train and develop newer talent in the current hybrid setting. Creating effective training and mentoring programmes in this environment requires greater intentionality and creativity amongst all of the players. Finding both in-person and digital opportunities to connect and learn will be needed to bring up the next cohort of lawyers.

Performance management is another area of focus. Emphasis on feedback and meaningful reviews – both upward and downward – is beneficial to everyone. When performance concerns do arise, having a thoughtful approach to managing next steps, whether that involves holding an associate back, providing coaching resources, or a soft landing for exits, is critical to maintaining a lasting bond and connection with these lawyers.

3. Do well at well-being and flexibility

Lawyers are struggling and we need to find ways to help. Mental health, substance abuse, burnout and pandemic trauma have left many legal professionals in a precarious state. And they are still hesitant to utilise firm resources to seek the help they need.

It is imperative that firms work to remove the stigma around mental health. The most effective strategy is top-down modelling from leadership. Leaders who are authentic and open about their own struggles and who prioritise healthy behaviour create a culture of transparency and support.

Psychosocial safety should be introduced into a firm's vocabulary, if it isn't already. Using this as a framework for making proactive decisions about how work is organised and performed will ensure that firm leaders are creating a safe, healthy and positive work culture for the entire workforce.

As firms construct and revise their return-to-office policies, keep in mind that flexibility is a key component of well-being. Employees who have more control of their work arrangements can better manage their stress levels and home obligations. Moreover, women and BIPOC prefer this arrangement.

4. Relationships, engagement and collegiality

Addressing the drop in motivation and fulfilment at law firms is crucial to cultivating a healthy law firm culture. Forming connections and creating a sense of belonging and purpose will help revive workforces that have emerged from the pandemic. Firms also need to be aware of the harmful exchanges and microaggressions that can occur virtually and are often difficult to detect.

Multiple generations in the workforce mean that there is a variety of life experiences and perspectives that are sometimes at odds with one another. Focusing on promoting empathy and psychological safety will ensure that each generation feels heard, understood and welcome. Leaders who are willing to adapt to individual preferences will find their workforce more content and engaged. Leaders should also encourage the generations to acknowledge one another's value and learn from each other.

5. DIB is still allowed – and important

Recent US Supreme Court decisions and private lawsuits have thrust affirmative action and DIB programmes into the spotlight once again; and many politicians are seizing the opportunity to politicise these efforts. It is critical that firms do not become distracted by this rhetoric, and focus on the innumerable benefits DIB brings not only to a firm's workforce, but its client retention and bottom line.

Given the significant representational disparities that remain, especially at the top, firms must stay committed to DIB efforts to have a real and lasting impact on their cultures. In particular, firms should focus on:

- the unintended consequences in-office mandates may have on marginalised groups, including women and caregivers;
- the importance of formalising and equalising work distribution;
- educating and expanding the notion of DIB for all generations;
- the data and whether a firm's policies and practices are producing meaningful change;
- reevaluating recruiting efforts to account for demographic shifts from the recent affirmative action rulings;
- using AI with caution; and
- ensuring the psychological and psychosocial safety of the entire workforce to create a sense of true belonging.

6. Recruiting and onboarding lessons

We'll keep saying it: law firms are a people business. A firm's ability to attract and retain top talent is essential to its success. Take care to consider how the firm is presenting itself – as firm culture is established at the outset. The efficiencies gained in recruiting through the use of virtual technology should be continued and encouraged. It saves time, reduces cost and significantly broadens the reach of candidates. Efforts are also going to be needed to re-recruit the current workforce to demonstrate the benefits of a long-term career at a law firm.

In the end, it is the firms where people trust and believe in the versatility and authenticity of their leaders – leaders who both safeguard and evolve their cultures – that will be strong enough to change, innovate and succeed in the face of any challenge, even a pandemic.

Culture is a daily practice.

Your brand will attract your best people.

Culture is the reason they walk through the door each morning.

Writing a brand book is not culture. In the same way, going to the gym in January is not fitness.

Perks is not culture.

Culture is not about spend.

Culture is what you do, not what you say you do.

Culture is not a slogan.

Culture is letting the wrong people go quickly.

Culture is not without pain.

Culture is sensing energy.

Culture is listening to what has not been said.

It is hard. And it is relentless.

Each day. Every day.

It is the hardest thing to keep. And the most important.

David Hieatt[586]

In the end, it is the firms where people trust and believe in the versatility and authenticity of their leaders – leaders who both safeguard and evolve their cultures – that will be strong enough to change, innovate and succeed in the face of any challenge, even a pandemic.

Notes

1 Xiumei Dong, "Why Better Law Firm Culture Must Come From The Top", *Law360 Pulse*, 22 June 2022, quoting Jarrett Green, law firm well-being and performance consultant.
2 Andrew Maloney, "'A Huge Concern': Big Law Leaders Grappling With Attorney Disengagement", *The American Lawyer*, 22 June 2023; Andrew Maloney, "Gen-Z Less Interested in Big Law and Traditional Law Firm Paths", *The American Lawyer*, 10 May 2023.
3 AJ Hess, "The professor who coined 'the Great Resignation' says it's finally over. Here's what's next", *Fast Company*, 3 August 2023.
4 Andrew Maloney, Patrick Smith and Hank Grezlak, "The Lawyers Are Not All Right", *The American Lawyer*, 30 January 2023.
5 Katherine B Forrest, "Cutting Through the Mess: What Does AI Really Mean for Lawyers?", *New York Law Journal*, 28 August 2023.
6 *Ibid.*
7 Jessie Yount, "Law Firms Race to Counsel Clients on AI—and Harness Those Learnings Internally", *The Recorder*, 30 August 2023.
8 Dan Packel, "O'Melveny's Brad Butwin on Managing in a Post-Pandemic Era," *The American Lawyer*, 28 August 2023.
9 Scott Westfahl, "How Firm Leaders Can Build And Sustain Culture", *Law360 Pulse*, 22 June 2022.
10 Emily Rose McRae, Peter Aykens, Kaelyn Lowmaster and Jonah Shepp, "9 Trends That Will Shape Work in 2023 and Beyond", *Harvard Business Review*, 18 January 2023.
11 Dan Packel, "O'Melveny's Brad Butwin on Managing in a Post-Pandemic Era", note 8.
12 Gary Burnison, Korn Ferry Special Edition email, "For the Love of the Game", 17 September 2023.
13 Korn Ferry, "Our time to take control: The future of work in 2023". Available at: www.kornferry.com/insights/featured-topics/future-of-work/future-workplace.
14 *Ibid.*
15 Andrew Maloney, "How the 2023 A-List Firms Manage to Holistic Success", *The American Lawyer*, 1 August 2023.
16 Xiumei Dong, "Why Better Law Firm Culture Must Come From The Top", *Law360 Pulse*, note 1.
17 Ben Grimes, "Leading With An Eye On Diversity", *ABA Law Practice Today*, 5 January 2023. Available at: www.lawpracticetoday.org/article/leading-with-an-eye-on-diversity/.
18 Sally Percy, "How Can Leaders Make Hybrid Working Work," *Forbes*, 5 April 2023, quoting Dr Debbie Bayntun-Lees, Professor of Organizational Change at Hult International Business School in the United Kingdom.
19 Deborah Perry Piscione and Josh Drean, "4 Forces That Are Fundamentally Changing How We Work", *Harvard Business Review*, 16 October 2023.
20 Sally Percy, "How Can Leaders Make Hybrid Working Work", referencing Dr Debbie Bayntun-Lees, note 18.
21 *Ibid.*
22 *Ibid.*
23 *Ibid*, referencing Dr David Liddle.
24 Patrick Smith, "Young Lawyers Want Ted Lasso As Their Leader, Not Bobby Knight", *The American Lawyer*, 3 May 2023.
25 Sally Percy, "How Can Leaders Make Hybrid Working Work", referencing Dr David Liddle note 18.
26 Paula Davis, "Forum: Strategies for effectively leading hybrid legal teams", *Thomson-Reuters*, 15 November 2022, www.thomsonreuters.com/en-us/posts/legal/forum-fall2022-leading-hybrid-legal-teams/.
27 Amanda O'Brien, "Cozen O'Connor Looks to Favor Officegoers in Work Allocation", *The Legal Intelligencer*, 26 September 2023. Heller also noted that: "But obviously client needs and services are top priority ... We will allocate work based primarily on who is best able to handle it."
28 Roberta Liebenberg, Paulette Brown and Stephanie Scharf, "Hybrid Work Policies: Key to the Recruitment, Retention of Women and Lawyers of Color", The Red Bee Group, 25 October 2021. Available at: www.theredbeegroup.com/wp-content/uploads/2020/02/Hybrid-Work-Policies-Key-to-the-Recruitment-Retention-of-Women-and-Lawyers-of-Color.pdf.
29 Emma Waldman, "How to Manage a Multi-Generational Team", *Harvard Business Review*, 31 August 2021.
30 Marcie Borgal Shunk, "How the Key to Engagement May Lie in Unlocking Generational Loyalties", *The Legal Intelligencer*, 18 May 2023.
31 Andrew Maloney, Patrick Smith and Hank Grezlak, "Generational Tensions Rise as Law Firms Move to Post-Pandemic Mode", *The American Lawyer*, 6 February 2023.
32 Marcie Borgal Shunk, "How the Key to Engagement May Lie in Unlocking Generational Loyalties", note 30.
33 *Ibid.*
34 Kevin Loria, Samantha Lee and Alexandra York, "Here's which generation you're part of based on your birth year — and why those distinctions exist", *Business Insider*, 29 May 2023.
35 Table 1 created by authors based on data from Purdue Global. Available at: https://imagine.jhu.edu/blog/2023/04/18/gen-z-in-the-workplace-how-should-companies-adapt/.
36 Vibha Sathesh Kumar, "Gen Z In The Workplace: How Should Companies Adapt?", John Hopkins University, 18 April 2023. Available at: https://imagine.jhu.edu/blog/2023/04/18/gen-z-in-the-workplace-how-should-companies-adapt/#:~:text=Today%2C%20a%20large%20chunk%20of,about%2030%25%20of%20the%20workforce.

37 Chris Cebollero, "How Leadership Has Changed Over Generations", *Forbes*, 14 March 2022.
38 *Ibid.*
39 Andrew Maloney *et al*, "Generational Tensions Rise as Law Firms Move to Post-Pandemic Mode", note 31.
40 *Ibid.*
41 *Ibid.*
42 *Ibid.*
43 *Ibid.*
44 "15 Ways Leaders Can More Effectively Manage Gen-Z Workers," *Forbes*, 17 January 2023.
45 *Ibid.*
46 *Ibid.*
47 *Ibid.*
48 Chris Cebollero, "How Leadership Has Changed Over Generations", note 37.
49 *Ibid.*
50 Stephen Mann, "Organizational Change Management – An Overview," ITSM Tools, 31 October 2019, https://itsm.tools/overview-of-organizational-change-management/ , citing *ITIL Practitioner Guidance*, The Stationery Office, 2016.
51 *Ibid.*
52 See the Kotter International website at: www.kotterinc.com/methodology/8-steps/.
53 *Ibid.*
54 *Ibid.*
55 Xiumei Dong, "Why Better Law Firm Culture Must Come From The Top", note 1.
56 Robert B Kaiser, Ryne A Sherman and Robert Hogan, "It Takes Versatility to Lead in a Volatile World", *Harvard Business Review*, 7 March 2023.
57 *Ibid.*
58 *Ibid.*
59 *Ibid.*
60 *Ibid.*
61 *Ibid.*
62 *Ibid.*
63 *Ibid.*
64 *Ibid.*
65 Table 2 created by authors based on data from Kaiser Leadership Solutions, Leadership Versatility and *Harvard Business Review*. Available at: https://hbr.org/data-visuals/2023/03/proportion-of-overall-leadership-effectiveness-related-to-versatility.
66 Wei Zheng, Jennifer Kim, Ronit Kark and Lisa Mascolo, "What Makes an Inclusive Leader?", *Harvard Business Review*, 27 September 2023.
67 *Ibid.*
68 *Ibid.*
69 Patrick Smith, "Young Lawyers Want Ted Lasso As Their Leader, Not Bobby Knight", note 24.
70 *Ibid.*
71 *Ibid.*
72 Dennis Kelly, "4 Insights From NLI's Psychological Safety Mini-Summit", NeoroLeadership Institute, 5 September 2023. Available at: https://neuroleadership.com/your-brain-at-work/4-insights-from-psych-safety-mini-summit.
73 *Ibid.*
74 *Ibid.*
75 *Ibid.*
76 Patrick Smith, "Young Lawyers Want Ted Lasso As Their Leader, Not Bobby Knight", note 24.
77 Juanita Kendall, "Seven Ways Law Firm Leaders Can Retain Talent", *Daily Report*, 6 June 2023.
78 Max Mitchell and Aleeza Furman, "Young Litigators Are More Demanding Than Ever. Firm Leaders Can Either Adapt or Bleed Talent", *The Legal Intelligencer*, 11 May 2023.
79 *Ibid.*
80 Jacob M Engel, "Why Does Culture 'Eat Strategy For Breakfast'", *Forbes*, 20 November 2018.
81 *Ibid.*
82 *Ibid.*
83 *Ibid.*
84 Sherilyn George-Clinton, "The Power of Choice", NeuroLeadership Institute, 13 October 2021, https://neuroleadership.com/your-brain-at-work/the-power-of-choice/.
85 Tracey Read, "Hogan Lovells' Next Global HR Pro On Getting And Keeping Talent", *Law360 Pulse*, 6 October 2023.
86 Ryan Gottfredson and Chris Reina, "To Be a Great Leader, You Need the Right Mindset", *Harvard Business Review*, 17 January 2020.
87 *Ibid.*
88 Ameet Ranadive, "Fixed v. Growth Mindset", *Medium*, 25 March 2016, https://medium.com/leadership-motivation-and-impact/fixed-v-growth-mindset-902e7d0081b3, quoting Carol Dweck in *Mindset: The New Psychology of Success*, Random House, 2007.
89 *Ibid.*
90 *Ibid.*
91 *Ibid.*

92 *Ibid.*
93 Breeann Webster, "How a Growth Mindset Shapes Leadership Skills", Dame Leadership, 19 April 2023, www.dameleadership.com/research-and-insights/how-a-growth-mindset-shapes-leadership-skills/.
94 *Ibid.*
95 *Ibid.*
96 Ameet Ranadive, "Fixed v. Growth Mindset", note 88.
97 *Ibid.*
98 Ryan Gottfredson and Chris Reina, "To Be a Great Leader, You Need the Right Mindset", note 86.
99 *Ibid.*
100 Breeann Webster, "How a Growth Mindset Shapes Leadership Skills", note 93.
101 Tara Parker-Pope, "The growth mind-set: Why friends, family and work make a difference", *The Washington Post*, 19 June 2023.
102 *Ibid.*
103 Anna Oakes, "How to develop a growth mindset in three steps", *Quartz*, 17 May 2023. Available at: https://qz.com/how-to-develop-a-growth-mindset-in-three-steps-1850444511.
104 *Ibid.*
105 *Ibid.*
106 Patrick Smith, "Young Lawyers Want Ted Lasso As Their Leader, Not Bobby Knight", note 24.
107 *Ibid.*
108 Juanita Kendall, "Seven Ways Law Firm Leaders Can Retain Talent", note 77.
109 *Ibid.*
110 Emma Waldman, "How to Manage a Multi-Generational Team," note 29.
111 Scott Westfahl, "How Firm Leaders Can Build And Sustain Culture", note 9.
112 Our time to take control, The future of work in 2023, Korn Ferry, www.kornferry.com/insights/featured-topics/future-of-work/future-workplace.
113 Scott Westfahl, "How Firm Leaders Can Build And Sustain Culture", note 9.
114 Korn Ferry, "Our time to take control: The future of work in 2023", note 13.
115 *Ibid.*
116 *Ibid.*
117 *Ibid.*
118 *Ibid.*
119 Scott Westfahl, "How Firm Leaders Can Build And Sustain Culture", note 9.
120 *Ibid.*
121 John Welsh, "7 Steps To Successful Succession Planning", *Forbes*, 14 January 2019. Available at: www.forbes.com/sites/johnwelsheurope/2019/01/14/7-steps-to-successful-succession-planning/.
122 *Ibid.*
123 *Ibid.*
124 Table 3, authors' own creation based on traditional 9-box potential/performance grid. See John Welsh, "7 Steps To Successful Succession Planning", *Forbes*, 14 January 2019. Available at: www.forbes.com/sites/johnwelsheurope/2019/01/14/7-steps-to-successful-succession-planning/.
125 *Ibid.*
126 Heather Smith, "Succession Planning During a Crisis: What you need to know now", DHR Global, 1 May 2020. Available at: www.dhrglobal.com/insights/succession-planning-during-crisis/.
127 Kristin Ryba, "The Complete Succession Planning Guide for HR Professionals", Quantum Workplace, 11 July 2023. Available at: www.quantumworkplace.com/future-of-work/the-importance-of-succession-planning.
128 Dentons, "Ensure a Strong Legacy With Succession Planning", 5 July 2022. Available at: www.dentons.com/en/insights/newsletters/2022/july/12/practice-tips-for-lawyers/ensure-a-strong-legacy-with-succession-planning.
129 *Ibid.*
130 *Ibid.*
131 *Ibid.*
132 *Ibid.*
133 Amanda O'Brien, "Closing of Two Law Firms Highlights Succession Planning Concerns", *The Legal Intelligencer*, 13 July 2023.
134 *Ibid.*
135 Ayse Yemiscigil, Dana Born and Horace Ling, "What Makes Leadership Development Programs Succeed?", *Harvard Business Review*, 28 February 2023.
136 *Ibid.*
137 *Ibid.*
138 *Ibid.*
139 *Ibid.*
140 Emily Rose McRae *et al*, "9 Trends That Will Shape Work in 2023 and Beyond", note 10.
141 Gina Passarella Cipriani, "Firms and Clients Worry Pandemic-Era Lawyers are Undertrained", *The Barometer*, 23 February 2023.
142 Jessie Yount, "Anxiety-Inducing Reviews May Hinder Law Firms' Training Efforts", *The American Lawyer*, 12 July 2023, quoting Sanford Michelman, chairman of Michelman & Robinson.
143 Jessie Yount, "Class Year Adjustments Underscore Lingering Skills Gap Among Associates", *The Recorder*, 24 April 2023.
144 Jessie Yount, "Anxiety-Inducing Reviews May Hinder Law Firms' Training Efforts", note 142.

145 Lian Parsons, "Why is Professional Development Important?", Harvard Division of Continuing Education blog, 23 August 2022. Available at: https://professional.dce.harvard.edu/blog/why-is-professional-development-important/.
146 Tom Sharbaugh, "Will remote work adversely affect the training, productivity, and retention of lawyers?", *Legal Evolution*, 17 July 2022.
147 Schmidt is quoted in Andrew Maloney, "In Era of Disengagement, How do Law Firms Motivate Lawyers and Staff", *The American Lawyer*, 26 June 2023.
148 *Ibid.*
149 *Ibid.*
150 Tom Sharbaugh, "Will remote work adversely affect the training, productivity, and retention of lawyers?", note 146.
151 *Ibid.*
152 *Ibid.*
153 *Ibid.*
154 Juanita Kendall, "Seven Ways Law Firm Leaders Can Retain Talent", note 77.
155 Amanda O'Brian, "In the Wake of Hybrid Work, Firms Get Creative in Using Their Space", *The Legal Intelligencer*, 28 July 2023.
156 *Ibid.*
157 Justin Henry and Jessie Yount, "Midsize Firms Scrutinize Sporadic Partner Attendance in Return to Office Push," *Pro Mid-Market*, 19 July 2023.
158 *Ibid.*
159 *Ibid.*
160 *Ibid.*
161 Emily Rose McRae *et al*, "9 Trends That Will Shape Work in 2023 and Beyond", note 10.
162 *Ibid.*
163 Gina Passarella Cipriani, "Firms and Clients Worry Pandemic-Era Lawyers are Undertrained", *The Barometer*, 23 February 2023.
164 Emily Rose McRae *et al*, "9 Trends That Will Shape Work in 2023 and Beyond", note 10.
165 *Ibid.*
166 *Ibid.*
167 Jeffrey A Lowe and Shannon K Murphy, "Millennials in Big Law: Resistance Is Futile", *The American Lawyer*, 7 January 2019.
168 *Ibid.*
169 Andrew Maloney, "More Millennial Lawyers Now Say They Want to Make Partner", *The American Lawyer*, 22 April 2023.
170 Jeffrey A Lowe and Shannon K Murphy, "Millennials in Big Law: Resistance Is Futile", note 167.
171 *Ibid.*
172 Trudy Knockless, "Desperate for Next Generation of Lawyers, Legal Departments Must Offer 'Meaningful Impact'", Law.com analysis, 4 April 2023.
173 *Ibid*, quoting Charlotte Smith, CEO of Level7 Legal.
174 Sally Sanderson, "Learning expectations of Millennials and Gen Z", Globe Law and Business blog, 14 September 2022. Available at: www.globelawandbusiness.com/blog/learning-expectations-of-millennials-and-gen-z.
175 Shunk, president and founder of The Tilt Institute, was quoted by Dan Roe in his article, "Returning to the Office Won't Get 'Zoom Associates' Back Up to Speed", *Pro Mid-Market*, 15 August 2023.
176 Dan Roe, "Returning to the Office Won't Get 'Zoom Associates' Back Up to Speed", *ibid*.
177 *Ibid.*
178 Laura Hilgers, "Boomers, Zoomers, Gen X, and Millennials: When It Comes to Learning, One Size Doesn't Fit All", LinkedIn Talent Blog, 24 April 2023. Available at: www.linkedin.com/business/talent/blog/learning-and-development/boomers-zoomers-gen-x-millennials-learning-styles.
179 *Ibid.*
180 *Ibid.*
181 *Ibid.*
182 *Ibid.*
183 *Ibid.*
184 *Ibid.*
185 *Ibid.*
186 Hasse Leonard-Pagel, "How to Attract, Develop, and Maintain Generationally Diverse Talent", Dilan Consulting Group Blog, 22 June 2022. Available at: https://dilanconsulting.com/how-to-attract-develop-and-maintain-generationally-diverse-talent/.
187 *Ibid.*
188 Masson is quoted in Andrew Maloney *et al*, "Generational Tensions Rise as Law Firms Move to Post-Pandemic Mode", note 31.
189 *Ibid.*
190 Cliff David and Barbara Steel, "How Focusing on Feedback Can Unlock Better Performance," NeuroLeadership Institute, 5 November 2020. Available at: https://neuroleadership.com/your-brain-at-work/better-feedback-unlock-performance/.
191 *Ibid.*
192 *Ibid.*

193 Ted Bauer, "Now Is the Perfect Time to Create a Culture of Asking for Feedback", NeuroLeadership Institute, 16 July 2020. Available at: https://neuroleadership.com/your-brain-at-work/create-a-culture-of-asking-for-feedback/.
194 Rachel Patterson, "Ghosting In BigLaw: Why Better Feedback Habits Are Needed", *Law360*, 3 May 2023.
195 *Ibid.*
196 Masson is quoted in Andrew Maloney *et al*, "Generational Tensions Rise as Law Firms Move to Post-Pandemic Mode", note 31.
197 Michael S Cohen was interviewed for an *Attorney at Work* editorial, "What Good Are Law Firm Performance Reviews?", 30 May 2022. Available at: www.attorneyatwork.com/what-good-are-law-firm-performance-reviews/#:~:text=They%20give%20the%20firm%20many,%2C%20attendance%2C%20behavior%20or%20attitude.
198 *Ibid.*
199 Diane Rosen and Laurie Lyte, "Making the Performance Review Process Better", *ABA Law Practice Today*, 14 January 2019. Available at: www.lawpracticetoday.org/article/making-performance-review-better/.
200 *Ibid.*
201 *Ibid.*
202 *Ibid.*
203 Patrick Smith, "How the Year-End Attorney Reviews Might Look a Little Different This Year", *The American Lawyer*, 20 November 2020.
204 Debra Cassens Weiss, "Hogan Lovells ditches annual performance reviews for program with 'flash feedback'", *ABA Journal*, 12 April 2018.
205 *Ibid.*
206 Jessie Yount, "Anxiety-Inducing Reviews May Hinder Law Firms' Training Efforts", note 142.
207 *Ibid.*
208 *Ibid*, quoting MLA legal recruiter Kate Reder Sheikh.
209 Paolo Confino, "Gen Z is so lacking in soft skills after lockdown that Big 4 consultants are offering classes to help new hires fit in at work", *Fortune*, 10 July 2023.
210 *Ibid.*
211 *Ibid.*
212 *Ibid.*
213 Scott Westfahl, "How Firm Leaders Can Build And Sustain Culture", note 9.
214 *Ibid.*
215 *Ibid.*
216 *Ibid.*
217 Gina Passarella Cipriani, "Firms and Clients Worry Pandemic-Era Lawyers are Undertrained", note 163.
218 *Ibid.*
219 Hasse Leonard-Pagel, "How to Attract, Develop, and Maintain Generationally Diverse Talent", note 186.
220 Schmidt is quoted in Andrew Maloney, "'A Huge Concern': Big Law Leaders Grappling With Attorney Disengagement", note 2.
221 *Ibid.*
222 Cate Galbally, "A Plea to Lawyers: Come Back to Pro Bono", *Support Center for Child Advocates*, 18 April 2022, https://sccalaw.org/a-plea-to-lawyers-come-back-to-pro-bono/.
223 Dan Bowman, "4 Reasons Lawyers Should Take on Pro Bono Cases", *National Law Review*, 29 June 2022, www.natlawreview.com/article/4-reasons-lawyers-should-take-pro-bono-cases.
224 Sally J Schmidt, "What Will Hybrid Marketing Look Like for Law Firms?", *Attorney at Work*, 28 May 2022. Available at: www.attorneyatwork.com/law-firms-hybrid-marketing/.
225 *Ibid.*
226 Erin R McClernon, "Practice Innovations: The evolution of the summer program during the pandemic", *Thomson Reuters*, 19 July 2022. Available at: www.thomsonreuters.com/en-us/posts/legal/practice-innovations-july22-summer-programs/.
227 *Ibid.*
228 *Ibid.*
229 Jessie Yount, "Class Year Adjustments Underscore Lingering Skills Gap Among Associates", note 143.
230 *Ibid.*
231 Patrick Krill, "Cracking the Code on Well-Being in Law: Applying Research and Experience to Advance an Essential but Elusive Priority", NALP *News & Journals*, May/June 2023.
232 *Ibid.*
233 Dan Roe, "'There's a Lot of Backlog to Address': Why Mental Health in the Legal Profession Is Getting Worse", *The American Lawyer*, 18 May 2023.
234 *Ibid.*
235 Dan Roe, "On Mental Health, Midsize Firms Trace Problems of Big Law", *Pro Mid-Market*, 13 June 2023.
236 Leah Brown, "'A Pressure Cooker': Mental Health is a Problem for In-House Lawyers Too", Law.com, 31 October 2022.
237 Bernie Wong and Kelly Greenwood, "The Future of Mental Health at Work Is Safety, Community, and a Healthy Organizational Culture", *Harvard Business Review*, 10 October 2023.

238 Emily Rose McRae *et al*, "9 Trends That Will Shape Work in 2023 and Beyond", note 10.
239 Andrew Maloney *et al*, "The Lawyers Are Not All Right", note 4.
240 Dan Roe, "'There's a Lot of Backlog to Address': Why Mental Health in the Legal Profession Is Getting Worse", note 233.
241 Ben Grimes, "Leading With An Eye On Diversity", note 17.
242 Patrick Krill, "Cracking the Code on Well-Being in Law: Applying Research and Experience to Advance an Essential but Elusive Priority", note 231.
243 Dan Roe, "Shifting Big Law Power Dynamics Pave Way for More 4-Day Attendance Policies", *The American Lawyer*, 8 June 2023.
244 Brenda Sapino Jeffreys, "'With Everybody Getting Back,' More Firms Want Lawyers in the Office", *The American Lawyer*, 21 June 2023.
245 Thomas Spigolon, "In Setting Office Attendance Policies, Southeast Law Firms Forge Their Own Paths", *Daily Report*, 28 July 2023.
246 *Ibid.*
247 Dan Roe, "Weil Gotshal to Require Four Days of Office Attendance", *The American Lawyer*, 22 July 2023.
248 Brenda Sapino Jeffreys, "Ropes' Move to 4 Days in the Office Includes International Offices", *The American Lawyer*, 1 August 2023.
249 *Ibid.*
250 Abigail Adcox, "Big Law Firms in DC 'Struggling' With How to Approach In-Office Policies", *National Law Journal*, 14 June 2023.
251 Jesse Yount, "'We Won't Mandate': West Coast Law Firms Aren't Following Wall Street Back to the Office", *The Recorder*, 19 July 2023.
252 *Ibid.*
253 *Ibid.*
254 *Ibid.*
255 Thomas Spigolon, "In Setting Office Attendance Policies, Southeast Law Firms Forge Their Own Paths", note 245.
256 Andrew Maloney, "In Era of Disengagement, How do Law Firms Motivate Lawyers and Staff", note 147.
257 *Ibid.*
258 Ashish Sareen, "Fried Frank Gives Remote Work Option To US And UK Staff", *Law360 Pulse*, 9 August 2023.
259 *Ibid.*
260 Jack Womack and Justin Henry, "Global Law Firms Are Finding 'Back to the Office' Means Different Things For Different People", Law.com, 19 September 2023.
261 Ashish Sareen, "Fried Frank Gives Remote Work Option To US And UK Staff", note 258.
262 *Ibid.*
263 *Ibid.*
264 Jack Womack and Justin Henry, "Global Law Firms Are Finding 'Back to the Office' Means Different Things For Different People", note 260.
265 *Ibid.*
266 *Ibid.*
267 *Ibid.*
268 *Ibid.*
269 *Ibid.*
270 Xiumei Dong, "Why Returning To The Office Isn't One-Size-Fits-All," *Law360 Pulse*, 31 July 2023.
271 Abigail Adcox, "As Pressure Grows for In-Office Mandates, Washington Law Firms Likely to Face 'Resistance'", *National Law Journal*, 7 August 2023.
272 Dan Roe, "Fear or FOMO: Big Law Split on How to Boost Office Attendance", *The American Lawyer*, 18 May 2023.
273 Jessie Yount, "Associates Frustrated by Unclear Expectations, Opacities in Return-to-Office Planning", *The Recorder*, 14 September 2023.
274 *Ibid.*
275 Jesse Yount, "'We Won't Mandate': West Coast Law Firms Aren't Following Wall Street Back to the Office", note 251.
276 *Ibid.*
277 Andrew Maloney, "The Office Has Gotten Better for Interaction, but Worse for Individual Work", *The American Lawyer*, 19 April 2023.
278 *Ibid.*
279 Jacob Zinkula and Juliana Kaplan, "Return to the office or see a pay cut: More and more companies are forcing remote workers to choose", *Business Insider*, 13 April 2023.
280 Dan Roe, "Fear or FOMO: Big Law Split on How to Boost Office Attendance", note 272.
281 Abigail Adcox, "Big Law Firms in DC 'Struggling' With How to Approach In-Office Policies", note 250.
282 Kevin Penton, "Firms Linking Associates' In-Office Attendance To Bonuses", *Law360 Pulse*, 30 May 2023.
283 Gretta Rusanow, Gloria Gomez and Scott Kesselman, "Law Firm Profits Soared In 2021, Despite Increased Expenses", Law.com, March 2022. Available at: www.lawjournalnewsletters.com/2022/03/01/law-firm-profits-soared-in-2021-despite-increased-expenses/?slreturn=20230924131927.

284 Amy Johnston, "Mental Health and Well-Being Challenges in Law Firms", *Practical Law – The Journal*, March 2023.
285 *Ibid.*
286 *Ibid.*
287 Amy Johnston, "Mental Health and Well-Being Challenges in Law Firms", note 284.
288 *Ibid.*
289 Beth Braccio Hering, "How Work Flexibility Can Improve Company Culture", FlexJobs, www.flexjobs.com/employer-blog/how-work-flexibility-can-improve-company-culture/.
290 Jeremie Brecheisen, "Research: Flexible Work Is Having a Mixed Impact on Employee Well-Being and Productivity", *Harvard Business Review*, 16 October 2023.
291 *Ibid.*
292 Patrick Krill, "Cracking the Code on Well-Being in Law: Applying Research and Experience to Advance an Essential but Elusive Priority", note 231.
293 *Ibid.*
294 Erin Hartley, "How to spot depression and anxiety in the remote workplace and help your employees", Meru Health. Available at: www.meruhealth.com/how-to-spot-depression-and-anxiety-in-the-remote-workplace-and-help-your-employees/#:~:text=Changes%20in%20presentation%3A%20Pay%20attention,be%20a%20sign%20of%20depression.
295 Dan Roe, "On Mental Health, Midsize Firms Trace Problems of Big Law", note 235.
296 "Gen-Z Attorneys Increasingly Aspire to Career Paths Beyond BigLaw, New Survey From MLA Finds", MLA Press Release, 10 May 2023. Available at: www.mlaglobal.com/en-gb/about-us/press-releases/gen-z-attorneys-increasingly-aspire-to-career-paths-beyond-biglaw-new-survey-from-mla-finds. The Gen Z Survey was conducted between January and March 2023, and surveyed law students and young lawyers from around the world, with a particular focus on those attending the top 100 law schools as ranked by U.S. News & World Report.
297 *Ibid.*
298 Andrew Maloney, "In Big Law, 'Flexibility' Is a Word for All Seasons", *The American Lawyer*, 14 August 2023.
299 *Ibid.*
300 Dan Roe, "In Battle for Billable Hours, Not Coming in Will Cost Some Associates Their Jobs", *The American Lawyer*, 30 May 2023.
301 *Ibid.*
302 One Mind at Work, *6th Annual One Mind at Work Global Forum Event Summary*, 13–14 September 2022. Available at: https://onemindatwork.org/wp-content/uploads/2022/11/2022-Global-Forum-Event-Summary_FINAL-1.pdf.
303 "Gen-Z Attorneys Increasingly Aspire to Career Paths Beyond BigLaw, New Survey From MLA Finds", note 296.
304 Dan Roe, "In Battle for Billable Hours, Not Coming in Will Cost Some Associates Their Jobs", note 300.
305 Catherine Collinson and Michael Hodin, "Best Practices for Engaging a Multigenerational Workforce", *Harvard Business Review*, 17 October 2023.
306 "Guide to Psychosocial Safety", NASP Blogger, 28 February 2023. Available at: https://naspweb.com/blog/guide-to-psychosocial-safety/.
307 Australian Public Service Commission, "Psychosocial safety", 19 May 2023. Available at: www.apsc.gov.au/initiatives-and-programs/aps-professional-streams/aps-hr-professional-stream/aps-hr-professional-news/psychosocial-safety.
308 *Ibid.*
309 Rianna Shanks, "Psychosocial safety requirements in the workplace", Employment Innovations, 29 March 2023. Available at: www.employmentinnovations.com/blog/psychosocial-safety-requirements-in-the-workplace/.
310 "Guide to Psychosocial Safety", NASP Blogger, note 306.
311 Dan Roe, "'There's a Lot of Backlog to Address': Why Mental Health in the Legal Profession Is Getting Worse", note 233.
312 *Ibid.*
313 *Ibid.*
314 "Guide to Psychosocial Safety", NASP Blogger, note 306.
315 Gavin Alexander, "Leading by Example: The Importance of Role Modeling for Lawyer Mental Health", ABA *Law Practice Today*, 5 January 2023. Available at: www.lawpracticetoday.org/article/leading-by-example-the-importance-of-role-modeling-for-lawyer-mental-health/.
316 Erica Coe, Jenny Cordina, Kana Enomoto and Nikhil Seshan, "Overcoming stigma: Three strategies toward better mental health in the workplace", *McKinsey Quarterly*, 23 July 2021. Available at: www.mckinsey.com/industries/healthcare/our-insights/overcoming-stigma-three-strategies-toward-better-mental-health-in-the-workplace.
317 Gavin Alexander, "Leading by Example: The Importance of Role Modeling for Lawyer Mental Health", note 315.
318 *Ibid* and Erica Coe *et al*, "Overcoming stigma: Three strategies toward better mental health in the workplace", note 316.
319 *Ibid.*

320 Megan Carnegie, "Is workplace stigma around mental health struggles changing?", BBC Worklife, 23 August 2022, referring to figures compiled by Mental Health First Aid England. Available at: www.bbc.com/worklife/article/20220819-is-workplace-stigma-around-mental-health-struggles-changing.
321 *Ibid.*
322 *Ibid.*
323 *Ibid.*
324 Table 4 created by authors using data from "National survey reveals disconnect between employees and employers around mental health need", McKinsey & Company, April 2021. Available at: www.mckinsey.com/~/media/mckinsey/industries/healthcare%20systems%20and%20services/our%20insights/national%20surveys%20reveal%20disconnect%20between%20employees%20and%20employers%20around%20mental%20health%20need/national-surveys-reveal-disconnect-around-mental-health.pdf.
325 Dr Kendall Browne, "Mental Health Stigma in the Workplace and How to Overcome it", Lyra Health. Available at: www.lyrahealth.com/resources/mental-health-stigma/.
326 *Ibid.*
327 *Ibid.*
328 Gavin Alexander, "Leading by Example: The Importance of Role Modeling for Lawyer Mental Health", note 315.
329 Dan Roe, "On Mental Health, Midsize Firms Trace Problems of Big Law," note 235.
330 One Mind at Work, *6th Annual One Mind at Work Global Forum Event Summary*, note 302.
331 Gavin Alexander, "Leading by Example: The Importance of Role Modeling for Lawyer Mental Health", note 315.
332 Dan Roe, "On Mental Health, Midsize Firms Trace Problems of Big Law", note 235.
333 Gavin Alexander, "Leading by Example: The Importance of Role Modeling for Lawyer Mental Health," note 315.
334 *Ibid.*
335 Dr Kendall Browne, "Mental Health Stigma in the Workplace (and How to Overcome it)," note 325.
336 Amy Johnston, "Mental Health and Well-Being Challenges in Law Firms", note 284.
337 *Ibid.*
338 Dr Kendall Browne, "Mental Health Stigma in the Workplace (and How to Overcome it)", note 325.
339 Amy Johnston, "Mental Health and Well-Being Challenges in Law Firms", note 284.
340 One Mind at Work, *6th Annual One Mind at Work Global Forum Event Summary*, note 302.
341 *Ibid.*
342 *Ibid.*
343 *Ibid.*
344 *Ibid.*
345 *Ibid.*
346 Patrick Krill, "Cracking the Code on Well-Being in Law: Applying Research and Experience to Advance an Essential but Elusive Priority", note 231.
347 *Ibid.*
348 Dan Roe, "'There's a Lot of Backlog to Address': Why Mental Health in the Legal Profession Is Getting Worse", note 233.
349 Brenda Sapino Jeffreys, "With Wellness at the Top of Mind, Law Firms Expand Support Resources", *The American Lawyer*, 9 February 2023.
350 *Ibid.*
351 Dan Roe, "On Mental Health, Midsize Firms Trace Problems of Big Law", note 235.
352 *Ibid.*
353 Drew Foster and Michelle Foster, "Work–Life Balance Vs. Competitive Pay: Which Matters More To Young Lawyers?", *Pro Mid-Market*, 23 June 2023.
354 *Ibid.*
355 Dan Roe, "The 1,800-Hour Year: Pipe Dream or Essential for Lawyers' Well-Being?", *The American Lawyer*, 27 July 2023.
356 *Ibid.*
357 *Ibid.*
358 *Ibid.*
359 Dan Roe, "'There's a Lot of Backlog to Address': Why Mental Health in the Legal Profession Is Getting Worse", note 233.
360 *Ibid.*
361 Dan Roe, "On Mental Health, Midsize Firms Trace Problems of Big Law", note 235.
362 Martindale-Avvo, "Work-Life Balance at Law Firms: Why It Matters And How to Achieve It", 13 December 2022. Available at: www.martindale-avvo.com/blog/work-life-balance-at-law-firms-why-it-matters-and-how-to-achieve-it/.
363 *Ibid.*
364 Hugo Guzman and Greg Andrews, "Study Finds Attorneys' Work–Life Balance Out of Kilter, With 42% Working on Weekends", *Corporate Counsel*, 11 October 2022.
365 *Ibid.*
366 "Work-Life Balance at Law Firms: Why It Matters And How to Achieve It", Martindale-Avvo, 13 December 2022. Available at: www.martindale-avvo.com/blog/work-life-balance-at-law-firms-why-it-matters-and-how-to-achieve-it/.

367 *Ibid.*
368 "Billable Hours May Never Go Away, but There's Room for Other Drivers of Performance", Law.com commentary, 3 October 2023.
369 *Ibid.*
370 Dan Roe, "'There's a Lot of Backlog to Address': Why Mental Health in the Legal Profession Is Getting Worse", note 233.
371 *Ibid.*
372 Eric Suni and Nilong Vyas, "How Lack of Sleep Impacts Cognitive Performance and Focus", Sleepfoundation.org, 18 July 2023. Available at: www.sleepfoundation.org/sleep-deprivation/lack-of-sleep-and-cognitive-impairment.
373 *Ibid.*
374 Eric Suni and Alex Dimitriu, "Sleep Deprivation: Understanding the Hidden Consequences", Sleepfoundation.org, 25 July 2023. Available at: www.sleepfoundation.org/sleep-deprivation.
375 Teresa Matich, "How to Challenge Norms and Build a Strong Law Firm Culture", Clio business blog post, 7 February 2022 Available at: www.clio.com/blog/law-firm-culture/.
376 Andrew Maloney, "In Era of Disengagement, How Do Law Firms Motivate Lawyers and Staff?", note 147.
377 AJ Hess, "The professor who coined 'the Great Resignation' says it's finally over. Here's what's next", note 3.
378 *Ibid.*
379 *Ibid.*
380 *Ibid.*
381 *Ibid.*
382 *Ibid.*
383 *Ibid.*
384 Kathleen Brady, "Build a Culture of Engagement," *Legal Management*. Available at: www.alanet.org/legal-management/2019/september/columns/build-culture-engagement.
385 Emily Rose McRae *et al*, "9 Trends That Will Shape Work in 2023 and Beyond", note 10.
386 Evan W Carr, Andrew Reece, Gabriella Rosen Kellerman and Alexi Robichaux, "The Value of Belonging at Work", *Harvard Business Review*, 16 December 2019.
387 Emma Seppälä and Marissa King, "Having Work Friends Can Be Tricky, but It's Worth It," *Harvard Business Review*, 8 August 2017.
388 *Ibid.*
389 Mark Mortensen, "Tension is Rising Around Remote Work", *Harvard Business Review*, 18 July 2023.
390 Marcie Borgal Shunk, "Pipe Dream of In-Office Demands: How to Enhance Engagement and Make a Hybrid Model Work", *The Legal Intelligencer*, 20 July 2023.
391 *Ibid.*
392 Justin Henry and Jessie Yount, "Midsize Firms Scrutinize Sporadic Partner Attendance in Return to Office Push", note 157.
393 Marcie Borgal Shunk, "Pipe Dream of In-Office Demands: How to Enhance Engagement and Make a Hybrid Model Work", note 390.
394 *Ibid.*
395 *Ibid.*
396 Tom Sharbaugh, "Will remote work adversely affect the training, productivity, and retention of lawyers?", note 146.
397 Mark Mortensen, "Why Hybrid Work Can Become Toxic", *Harvard Business Review*, 28 July 2023.
398 *Ibid.*
399 *Ibid.*
400 *Ibid.*
401 *Ibid.*
402 Ella F Washington, "Recognizing and Responding to Microaggressions at Work", *Harvard Business Review*, 10 May 2022.
403 *Ibid.*
404 *Ibid.*
405 *Ibid.*
406 *Ibid.*
407 *Ibid.*
408 Adam Grant, organisational psychologist and professor of management at The Wharton School, Twitter post, 13 June 2023. Available at: https://twitter.com/AdamMGrant/status/1668679477742673944?lang=en.
409 Thomson Reuters Institute and the Georgetown Law Center on Ethics and the Legal Profession, *2023 Report on the State of the Legal Market*, p18. Available at: www.thomsonreuters.com/en-us/posts/wp-content/uploads/sites/20/2023/01/2023-State-of-the-Legal-Market.pdf.
410 Marcie Borgal Shunk, "Pipe Dream of In-Office Demands: How to Enhance Engagement and Make a Hybrid Model Work", note 390.
411 *Ibid.*
412 *Ibid.*
413 Marcie Borgal Shunk, "How the Key to Engagement May Lie in Unlocking Generational Loyalties", note 30.

414 *Ibid.*
415 *Ibid.*
416 *Ibid.*
417 Marcie Borgal Shunk, "Pipe Dream of In-Office Demands: How to Enhance Engagement and Make a Hybrid Model Work", note 390.
418 Nicole de Fontaines, executive director of CEMS at The Global Alliance in Management Education, quoted in Sally Percy, "How Can Leaders Make Hybrid Working Work", note 18.
419 *Ibid.*
420 Marcie Borgal Shunk, "How the Key to Engagement May Lie in Unlocking Generational Loyalties", note 30.
421 *Ibid.*
422 Ann Gomez and Myriah Graves, "Top 4 Concerns about Hybrid Work and How Legal Teams are Responding", Clear Concept Inc, 2 September 2022. Available at: https://clearconceptinc.ca/wp-content/uploads/2022/09/NALP-Bulletin-September-2022_-Ann-Gomez-and-Myriah-Graves_-Top-4-concerns-about-hybrid-work.pdf.
423 Mark Mortensen, "Why Hybrid Work Can Become Toxic", *Harvard Business Review*, 28 July 2023.
424 *Ibid.*
425 *Ibid.*
426 Andrew Maloney, "Return to Office Is a Focus For Mentoring, but Training Gaps Have Existed for Ages", *The American Lawyer*, 12 June 2023.
427 *Ibid.*
428 Emily Rose McRae *et al*, "9 Trends That Will Shape Work in 2023 and Beyond", note 10.
429 Marcie Borgal Shunk, "Pipe Dream of In-Office Demands: How to Enhance Engagement and Make a Hybrid Model Work", note 390.
430 *Ibid.*
431 *Ibid.*
432 *Ibid.*
433 Mckinsey & Company, "What is diversity, equity, and inclusion?", 17 August 2022. Available at: www.mckinsey.com/featured-insights/mckinsey-explainers/what-is-diversity-equity-and-inclusion.
434 *Ibid.*
435 LaFawn Davis, "How Belonging Differs from Diversity and Inclusion—and Why It Matters", Indeed, 2 September 2020. Available at: https://ca.indeed.com/leadershiphub/how-belonging-differs-from-diversity-and-inclusion.
436 ABA, *Profile of the Legal Profession*, 2023. Available at: www.americanbar.org/content/dam/aba/administrative/news/2023/potlp-2023.pdf.
437 *Ibid.*
438 Sarah Martinson, "DEI Efforts Falling Short For Many Black Women Attorneys", *Law360 Pulse*, 4 August 2023.
439 *Ibid.*
440 Angela Winfield, "We Must Continue DEI Efforts Despite High Court Headwinds", *Law360 Pulse*, 26 July 2023.
441 *Ibid.*
442 Tina Opie and Ella F Washington, "Why Companies Can – and Should – Recommit to DEI in the Wake of the SCOTUS Decision", *Harvard Business Review*, 27 July 2023.
443 *Ibid.*
444 *Ibid.*
445 Dan Roe, "Blum Lawsuits Stress-Test Law Firms' DEI Commitment, Execution", *The American Lawyer*, 14 September 2023. David Thomas, "Winston & Strawn is latest US law firm sued over diversity programs", *Reuters*, 30 October 2023.
446 *Ibid.*
447 *Ibid.*
448 Tina Opie and Ella F Washington, "Why Companies Can – and Should – Recommit to DEI in the Wake of the SCOTUS Decision", note 442.
449 Wei Zheng et al, "What Makes an Inclusive Leader?", note 66.
450 Tina Opie and Ella F Washington, "Why Companies Can – and Should – Recommit to DEI in the Wake of the SCOTUS Decision", note 442.
451 *Ibid.*
452 Curtis L Odom, Jennifer Franczak and Charn P McAllister, "Equity in the Hybrid Office", *MIT Sloan Management Review*, 24 March 2022.
453 Amanda O'Brian, "Push to 4-Day Attendance Poses Risks for Law Firm Diversity Efforts", *The Intelligencer*, 9 June 2023.
454 *Ibid.*
455 *Ibid.*
456 *Ibid.*
457 Tom Sharbaugh, "Will remote work adversely affect the training, productivity, and retention of lawyers?", note 146.
458 "Diversity and Inclusion in the Workplace by Generation", DallasHR blog, 7 July 2020. Available at: https://blog.dallashr.org/diversity-and-inclusion-in-the-workplace-by-generation/.
459 *Ibid.*
460 *Ibid.*

461 *Ibid.*
462 Monster.com, "What workforce diversity means for Gen Z". Available at: https://hiring.monster.com/resources/workforce-management/diversity-in-the-workplace/workforce-diversity-for-millennials/.
463 "Diversity and Inclusion in the Workplace by Generation", note 458.
464 Christie Smith and Stephanie Turner, "The Radical Transformation of Diversity and Inclusion The Millennial Influence", Deloitte University Leadership Center for Inclusion, 2015. Available at: www2.deloitte.com/content/dam/Deloitte/us/Documents/about-deloitte/us-inclus-millennial-influence-120215.pdf.
465 *Ibid.*
466 Diversity and Inclusion in the Workplace by Generation", note 458.
467 *Ibid.*
468 *Ibid.*
469 *Ibid.*
470 *Ibid.*
471 Jennifer Miller, "For younger job seekers, diversity and inclusion in the workplace aren't a preference. They're a requirement", *The Washington Post*, 18 February 2021.
472 *Ibid.*
473 Lily Zheng, "How to Effectively – and Legally – Use Racial Data for DEI", *Harvard Business Review*, 24 July 2023.
474 Table 5 adapted from figure featured in "Where are you on the D&I maturity curve?", PwC, 17 December 2018. Available at: www.pwc.com/us/en/industries/industrial-products/library/diversity-inclusion-maturity-curve.html.
475 Tina Opie and Ella F Washington, "Why Companies Can – and Should – Recommit to DEI in the Wake of the SCOTUS Decision", note 442.
476 Kevin Penton, "DEI Roundup: 3 Lessons For Law Firms", *Law360 Pulse*, 27 July 2023.
477 Tina Opie and Ella F Washington, "Why Companies Can – and Should – Recommit to DEI in the Wake of the SCOTUS Decision", note 442.
478 *Ibid.*
479 Pulsely, "5 Ways to Become More Conscious About Systemic Bias". Available at: https://pulsely.io/blog/5-ways-to-become-more-conscious-about-systemic-bias#:~:text=According%20to%20Oxford%20Reference%2C%20systemic,others%20being%20disadvantaged%20or%20devalued.
480 Adwoa Bagalini, "Three cognitive biases perpetuating racism at work – and how to overcome them", World Economic Forum, 19 August 2020. Available at: www.weforum.org/agenda/2020/08/cognitive-bias-unconscious-racism-moral-licensing/.
481 *Ibid.*
482 Misha Gajewski, "You're More Racist Than You Think: How Your Mental Biases Perpetuate Racism And How To Fix Them", *Forbes*, 29 June 2020.
483 Tina Opie and Ella F Washington, "Why Companies Can – and Should – Recommit to DEI in the Wake of the SCOTUS Decision", note 442.
484 Kevin Penton, "DEI Roundup: 3 Lessons For Law Firms", note 476.
485 Dan Roe, "Gibson Dunn Forms DEI Task Force as Employers Rush to Comply With Affirmative Action Reversal", *The American Lawyer*, 20 July 2023.
486 *Ibid.*
487 Michele Gorman, "GCs Really Want To Help Firms Improve On Diversity", *Law360 Pulse*, 26 July 2023.
488 *Ibid.*
489 Anna Helhoski, "AI Could Prevent Hiring Bias — Unless It Makes It Worse", NerdWallet, 12 June 2023. Available at: www.nerdwallet.com/article/finance/ai-hiring-decisions.
490 *Ibid.*
491 *Ibid.*
492 Jonathan Kestenbaum, "NYC's New AI Bias Law Broadly Impacts Hiring and Requires Audits", *Bloomberg Law*, 5 July 2023.
493 *Ibid.*
494 Xiumei Dong, "Why Better Law Firm Culture Must Come From The Top", note 1.
495 *Ibid.*
496 *Ibid.*
497 Samantha Stokes, "Meet 7 diversity leaders who are fighting for equality and inclusion in Big Law at firms like Baker McKenzie and White & Case", *Business Insider*, 5 February 2021.
498 LaFawn Davis, "How Belonging Differs from Diversity and Inclusion – and Why It Matters", note 435.
499 *Ibid.*
500 *Ibid.*
501 Kevin Penton, "DEI Roundup: 3 Lessons For Law Firms", note 476.
502 *Ibid.*
503 *Ibid.*
504 Kenji Yoshino and David Glasgow, "What SCOTUS's Affirmative Action Decision Means for Corporate DEI", *Harvard Business Review*, 12 July 2023.
505 *Ibid.*

506 Lauren Morgan Roberts, "Where Does DEI Go from Here?", *Harvard Business Review*, 14 September 2023.
507 *Ibid.*
508 *Ibid.*
509 *Ibid.*
510 *Ibid.*
511 *Ibid.*
512 *Ibid.*
513 *Ibid.*
514 *Ibid.*
515 Bernie Wong and Kelly Greenwood, "The Future of Mental Health at Work Is Safety, Community, and a Healthy Organizational Culture", note 237.
516 Ekansh, "Law Firm Recruitment Best Practices To Win The Talent War," *Aspioneer*, 11 August 2022. Available at: https://aspioneer.com/law-firm-recruitment-best-practices-to-win-the-talent-war/.
517 *Ibid.*
518 *Ibid.*
519 Ronald Nye, Tina Cohen Nicol, Heather Fine and Allison LaFramboise, "The Legal Hiring Market Forecast for 2023", MLA Insights, 29 March 2023. Available at: www.mlaglobal.com/en/insights/articles/the-legal-hiring-market-forecast-for-2023.
520 *Ibid.*
521 Amanda Robert, "Working remotely is now a top priority, says new ABA report highlighting lasting shifts in practice of law", *ABA Journal*, 28 September 2022. Red Bee Group designed and managed the ABA survey.
522 *Ibid.*
523 *Ibid.*
524 Drew Foster and Michelle Foster, "Work–Life Balance Vs. Competitive Pay: Which Matters More To Young Lawyers?", note 353.
525 *Ibid.*
526 Dan Packel, "From Six Months to Six Weeks: Lateral Hiring Is Speeding Up", *The American Lawyer*, 29 July 2020.
527 *Ibid.*
528 *Ibid.*
529 Justin Henry, "Large Lateral Moves Are Raising the Competitive Ante for Law Firms", *The American Lawyer*, 15 May 2023.
530 *Ibid.*
531 *Ibid.*
532 *Ibid.*
533 *Ibid.*
534 *Ibid.*
535 *Ibid.*
536 *Ibid.*
537 Andrew Maloney, Patrick Smith and Hank Grezlak, "Generational Tensions Rise as Law Firms Move to Post-Pandemic Mode", note 31.
538 "Gen-Z Attorneys Increasingly Aspire to Career Paths Beyond BigLaw, New Survey From MLA Finds", note 296.
539 *Ibid.*
540 *Ibid.*
541 *Ibid.*
542 *Ibid.*
543 Andrew Maloney *et al*, "The Lawyers Are Not All Right", note 4.
544 Alina Veselaya, "Generational theory in corporate learning: how to do training for Gen Z, Y, X, and Boomers", My Learning Hub blog, 13 July 2022. Available at: https://mylearninghub.com/blog/post/generational-theory-corporate-learning.
545 "Gen-Z Attorneys Increasingly Aspire to Career Paths Beyond BigLaw, New Survey From MLA Finds", note 296.
546 Andrew Maloney *et al*, "The Lawyers Are Not All Right", note 4.
547 Alina Veselaya, "Generational theory in corporate learning: how to do training for Gen Z, Y, X, and Boomers", note 544.
548 Andrew Maloney, "'A Huge Concern': Big Law Leaders Grappling With Attorney Disengagement", note 2.
549 Matt Perez, "What Do Young Attorneys Want? Transparency, Flexibility", *Law360 Pulse*, 20 January 2023.
550 Andrew Maloney, "'A Huge Concern': Big Law Leaders Grappling With Attorney Disengagement", note 2.
551 *Ibid.*
552 *Ibid.*
553 AJ Hess, "The professor who coined 'the Great Resignation' says it's finally over. Here's what's next", note 3.
554 Andrew Maloney, "'A Huge Concern': Big Law Leaders Grappling With Attorney Disengagement", note 2.

555 *Ibid.* Referencing Paul Schmidt, chair of BakerHostetler.
556 Duane Cormell, "Legal Recruitment: A Legal Recruiter's Guide to Attracting the Best Talent", Clio Blog, 4 November 2022. Available at: www.clio.com/uk/blog/legal-recruitment-attracting-talent/.
557 Amanda Robert, "Working remotely is now a top priority, says new ABA report highlighting lasting shifts in practice of law", note 521.
558 *Ibid.*
559 *Ibid.*
560 *Ibid.*
561 Steve Nelson, "Recruiting and Retention: Seven Strategies to Help Win the War for Talent", *Attorney at Work*, 5 July 2023. Available at www.attorneyatwork.com/seven-strategies-law-firm-recruiting-and-retention/.
562 *Ibid.*
563 *Ibid.*
564 Duane Cormell, "Legal Recruitment: A Legal Recruiter's Guide to Attracting the Best Talent", note 556.
565 "What makes lawyers happy? Keys to attract and retain talent in 2023," Thomson Reuters, 22 February 2023, https://legal.thomsonreuters.com/blog/keys-to-attract-and-retain-top-legal-talent/.
566 *Ibid.*
567 *Ibid.*
568 Jessie Yount, "Flexibility Is a Talent Attractor, But It Comes With Its Own Challenges", *The American Lawyer*, 5 September 2023.
569 Andrew Maloney, "Young Lawyers Are Willing to Sacrifice Their Comp for These Benefits", *The American Lawyer*, 23 April 2023.
570 *Ibid.*
571 Tracy LaLonde, "Wellness Initiatives Are Nice, but They Aren't Solving the Root Problem: Engagement", Law.com, 11 September 2023.
572 Steve Nelson, "Recruiting and Retention: Seven Strategies to Help Win the War for Talent", note 561.
573 *Ibid.*
574 Amanda Robert, "Working remotely is now a top priority, says new ABA report highlighting lasting shifts in practice of law", note 521.
575 *Ibid.*
576 Drew Foster and Michelle Foster, "Work–Life Balance Vs. Competitive Pay: Which Matters More To Young Lawyers?", note 353.
577 Amy Johnston, "Mental Health and Well-Being Challenges in Law Firms", note 284.
578 Drew Foster and Michelle Foster, "Work–Life Balance Vs. Competitive Pay: Which Matters More To Young Lawyers?", note 353.
579 *Ibid.*
580 *Ibid.*
581 Dan Roe, "1 in 4 Big Law Associates Plan to Leave Within the Year", *The American Lawyer*, 10 October 2023.
582 *Ibid.*
583 Dan Roe, "'Stay Interviews' Help Law Firms Adjust to Young Lawyers' Changing Needs", *The American Lawyer*, 11 August 2023.
584 Dan Roe, "1 in 4 Big Law Associates Plan to Leave Within the Year", note 581.
585 Andrew Maloney, "How the 2023 A-List Firms Manage to Holistic Success", *The American Lawyer*, 1 August 2023.
586 David Hieatt, co-founder of Hiut Denim Co, LinkedIn Post. Available at: www.linkedin.com/posts/davidhieatt_cosmicantlers100-culture-brandstrategy-activity-6955982031273005056-vQ9c/?trk=public_profile_like_view&originalSubdomain=uk.

About the authors

Naomi Beard Nelson
Founder and CEO, Beard Strategies, Inc
naomi@beardstrategies.com

Naomi Beard Nelson has been a leader in law firm consulting and executive coaching for over 17 years. Following a decade of practising law in large law firms, she shifted focus to consulting and coaching. Naomi helps firms optimise their talent development, engagement and retention strategies. With deep insight into the shared challenges faced by today's top law firms, she advances change at the individual and organisational level. Her instinct for tapping into each client's strengths and needs enables them to surmount sizeable obstacles to realise ambitious goals.

Naomi is immersed in cutting-edge topics like hybrid work, building resilient firm cultures, developing leaders, designing retention strategies and advancing inclusion and well-being. Her approach is collaborative, incisive and rooted in up-to-the-minute market intelligence. Her clients count on her to go the extra mile and attain world-class outcomes.

Mary Ellen Connerty
President, ME Connerty Consulting
meconnerty@gmail.com

Mary Ellen Connerty has over 30 years of experience leading talent development in professional services consultancies and law firms. A proven leader in diversity, equity and inclusion (DE&I), talent development systems, leadership growth and culture-building initiatives, she is also a seasoned human capital consultant.

Most recently, Mary Ellen spent 10 years at O'Melveny & Myers, leading its DE&I and engagement efforts. She successfully grew the ranks of women and attorneys of colour through innovative recruiting and retention programmes, including new assessment tools that help eliminate bias, an inaugural engagement survey, diversity-specific professional development retreats and an analysis of systemic bias. During her tenure, the firm was repeatedly recognised for its DE&I achievements by organisations like Great Place to Work, Working Mother, Chambers, the Human Rights Campaign, AmLaw and Vault.

Michelle Egan
President, JME Advisors
michelle@jmeadvisors.com

With over 30 years of experience as a law firm business professional, Michelle Egan helps firms optimise their talent development programmes, retention strategies, human resources initiatives and organisational cultures. Michelle's work with large firms – both in the United States and abroad – has given her a keen understanding of organisational behaviour and the business challenges unique to the legal industry.

About Globe Law and Business

Globe Law and Business was established in 2005. From the very beginning, we set out to create legal books that are sufficiently high level to be of real use to the experienced professional, yet still accessible and easy to navigate. Most of our authors are drawn from Magic Circle and other top commercial firms, both in the United Kingdom and internationally.

Our titles are carefully produced, with the utmost attention paid to editorial, design and production processes. We hope this results in high-quality publications that are easy to read and a pleasure to own.

In 2021, we were very pleased to announce the start of a new chapter for Globe Law and Business following the acquisition of law books under the imprint Ark Publishing. Our law firm management list is now significantly expanded with many well known and loved Ark Publishing titles.

We are also pleased to announce the launch of our online content platform, Globe Law Online. This allows for easy search and networked access across firms. Key collections include the Law Firm Management Collection (including a module on Strategy and Management). Details of all titles included can be found at www.globelawonline.com. Email glo@globelawandbusiness.com for further details and to arrange a free trial for you or your firm.

We'd very much like to hear from you with your thoughts and ideas for improving what we offer. Please do feel free to email me on sian@globelawandbusiness.com. Happy reading and thank you for your time.

Sian O'Neill
Managing director
Globe Law and Business
www.globelawandbusiness.com

Milton Keynes UK
Ingram Content Group UK Ltd.
UKHW050846140524
442596UK00002B/3

9 781787 429284